BRILLIANT,
BEAUTIFUL,
BIPOLAR

Liz Casper

Available as an ebook

ISBN 979-8-9928998-3-2 (paperback)

ISBN 979-8-2822983-8-3 (hardcover)

Publify Publishing

Lampasas, TX 76550

contact@publifypublishing.com

LizCasper.com

To Elon Musk

If it weren't for Elon's appearance on *Saturday Night Live* and subsequent admission of his Asperger's, I would not have ever released this book. His courage to share his diagnosis inspired me to share my own diagnosis and story. I hope you find it of interest and maybe of help.

Author's Note and Disclaimer

This book details my story of my diagnosis of a serious and potentially fatal illness, bipolar disorder. I have decided to write this story now, painful as reliving some of the history is, to provide inspiration and information to others currently struggling with an illness and to their families and loved ones who care about them. I do not intend this piece to replace the advice of physicians or health care practitioners; nor am I intending to diagnose or prescribe treatment for any illness or disorder. It is my personal story only.

If you are suffering from any medical condition, you should seek qualified professional attention before beginning, changing, or ending any regimen of medicine, nutrition, or supplements.

Table of Contents

Prologue

The first thing you should know is that I avoided writing this book for several years until I could get some distance and perspective regarding all I have been through, as chronicled in this book. The next thing you need to know is that I did not title this book myself; my mom did. I decided to use this title because I liked the alliteration, not because I have bought into the idea that I am brilliant and/or beautiful. But I am bipolar, so the title stuck.

I wrote this book to give insight and perspective into a disease that affects at least three percent of our population in the United States and over thirty million people worldwide. What many do not know is that fully fifty percent of our population may be diagnosed with a mental health illness in their lifetime. With little being written on the subject for laypeople and even less written from the perspective of someone actively manic and unroofed, I offer you this story.

My wish is that you will gain an understanding of the world of someone suffering from unmedicated and medicated bipolar disorder (BPD). Now that I am stable on medication, it is, quite literally, what keeps me both alive and on an even keel. I hope you benefit from what I have written and perhaps gain a new insight into this affliction.

Chapter 1

The Beginning

As a child, I never felt that I fit in. It was a lonely childhood marred by tragedy and trauma. At age seven, my mother, younger brother, and I were involved in a ninety-mile-per-hour head-on impact collision with another car. My brother, a tiny, adorable four-year-old, was killed instantly but then resuscitated at the scene with tragic consequences. I was seven years old and badly injured as well, with significant injuries, including a serious head injury, crossed eyes, ruptured colon, broken back, and a destroyed face. The scars and memories from that day as I witnessed the resuscitation of my brother, have stayed with me to this day.

The year was 1972, and in the decades that followed, I would often relive that traumatic experience—night terrors, daytime flashbacks, and so forth. The term post-traumatic stress disorder (PTSD) was not discussed back then, especially if you hadn't been in military combat. I knew something was deeply wrong in my mind, but I did not know what it was or how to deal with it. I was diagnosed with depression several times over the decades, but the medications did little to help my suffering, and oftentimes, I felt the medication made me feel worse. I managed to mostly suppress my PTSD and live a somewhat normal life until the wheels started to come off in my late forties.

At age fifteen, my father told me that I needed to go to an Ivy League school for college. I accepted that pressure and spent my high school years preparing for admission. Once there, three thousand miles from my hometown, I did my best to like the business program I was in. But after a year, I dropped out and decided to find a career doing something else.

I had met a man at the Ivy League who would later become my first husband. After I dropped out and he graduated, we stayed on the East Coast, and I began a rewarding career in New York City working for one of the world's iconic fashion and beauty houses. I loved my life in New York City and wanted to continue, but after five years of gratifying work, I realized I had hit the glass ceiling. I wouldn't be able to advance my career without that college degree. (Remember, this was 1989, and the rules were different then.)

My husband and I decided to both go back to school, he for a law degree and I for completion of my undergraduate degree. We moved to the West Coast and established our new life together. I attended a liberal arts college and decided on a bachelor's degree in science, with a major in art. This unconventional combination of science and art fit me perfectly. One day, my art thesis advisor told me that I wasn't good at drawing, a true story still to this day, and she suggested I take an anatomy class to learn how to draw the human body better.

On my first day of anatomy class, I walked into the lab and had a lightbulb moment. Although I hailed from a medical family with three generations of physicians before me, I had never considered medicine for myself. In my family of origin, medicine was reserved for men. In fact, my younger brother, the one massively injured in our car accident, had a medical school trust fund, but I did not. Regardless, on that first day of anatomy, I knew I had found my new purpose in life: I would become a medical doctor.

Chapter 2
On Doctoring

I spent the next eighteen months of college taking science prerequisites and getting prepared for medical school. I applied to only one school and was accepted. The next eight years were a whirlwind of medical school, internship, residency, and starting a family. I had two sons while in medical school, which made the whole experience simultaneously much harder and much more rewarding. My husband had become a practicing attorney, and we soon realized that our two careers—and we—had become incompatible. Our acrimonious divorce, combined with my demanding medical career, really took its toll on my psyche.

I was desperate to have a stable relationship and got married again soon after meeting another attorney. (I've since sworn off attorneys for good!) I think we both knew we weren't compatible, but we took the plunge anyway. Within a year, I realized what a mistake I had made, but it took another six years for us to part ways. Once we decided to divorce, my husband took his clothes and walked out of our lives without so much as a goodbye. My children were devastated, and so was I at the reality of a second failed marriage.

My children's father and I shared custody of our two boys. One night after my second divorce, I had the evening alone without my kids. I felt like a complete failure and couldn't see a future for myself. I decided it was time to commit suicide. I went into my garage and prepared my new, white Mercedes SL550 for the job.

I showered, fixed my hair, put on makeup, and dressed in an all-white suit. I had decided that the best way to leave was while wearing white, sitting in a white car inside a white house's garage. It seemed maudlin and poetic, and I hoped the person(s) finding me would get it. The all-white theme was in stark contrast to the darkness inside of me.

Before I turned on the car to idle, I decided to have (another) glass of wine. I sat on my white couch with my white wine and sobbed. Life seemed so bleak, and death seemed so alluring. But as luck would have it, I had one too many glasses of wine and fell fast asleep on the couch. I woke up the next morning very unhappy with the outcome. I couldn't believe it. I was such a failure that I had failed at killing myself. I lacked the energy to try again, so I packed the plan away into the recesses of my mind and carried on with my life.

Chapter 3
Trouble Begins

I continued my career as a physician and my role as a single mother. It was difficult, agonizing at times, and the stress was reaching a crescendo. Physically, I was overworked, overfed, under-exercised, and mentally and emotionally drained. I needed to change my life, but didn't know how. I was trapped in a never-ending cycle of pain, overwhelm, and stress.

One night, I went to a charity event with one of my employees. Outwardly, we had a great time at the event—eating great food and drinking too much alcohol—but inwardly, I felt alone, lonely, and anxious. Toward the end of the evening, my employee and I were approached by the event coordinator, who told both of us she did not think we should drive home. She offered a cab to get home. (Uber and Lyft didn't exist at that time.)

My employee said yes to the ride home, but I said, "No thanks."

As the event was in a hotel, I let the lady know I would just stay at the hotel overnight rather than take the long cab ride home. I told her

I needed to get a few things out of my car before checking in. I had just purchased a new, white Mercedes SUV, and I wanted to move it closer to the hotel entrance for safekeeping.

I exited the hotel and walked the distance to my car. I drove the car less than a hundred feet to the hotel entrance and began to gather my things to stay the night.

Chapter 4
The Beginning of the End

I took an armload of my stuff from the car and walked with a limp back into the hotel to register. As I did, a police officer greeted me. Tall and bulky, he had a very serious look on his face.

"Excuse me. Are you Liz?" he asked.

"Yes, that's me," I replied.

"I understand you've been drinking tonight," he continued.

"Yes, I have been drinking," I said.

"And I understand you've been driving?" he asked.

"No, I'm not driving, which is why I'm checking into the hotel," I replied.

"You were seen moving your car in the hotel parking lot," he stated.

I really didn't know how to respond to that and realized I was being set up. "I did move my car to a safer location, so if that's considered driving, then I did drive."

What happened next is a blur. As soon as I finished my sentence, the cop pulled out handcuffs, slapped them on me in the hotel lobby, and read me my Miranda rights. I noticed the charity coordinator watching the whole episode with glee. I literally thought she was going to clap. I was taken to the central precinct and booked for DUI.

When you are arrested, you get one phone call, but not your phone. This means you better remember someone's number! The only adult phone number I could recall was my recent ex-husband's. I called him at four o'clock in the morning, and he graciously picked me up and took me back to my car.

The next morning, my mug shot came out on the internet, and a vengeful former employee kindly sent my mug shot to the Washington Board of Medical Examiners, commencing the beginning of the end of my medical career.

The result of the DUI was that I couldn't drive for ninety days. Then I had to install a Breathalyzer in my new car for a year. It seemed incredibly unfair, as I thought I had been doing the right thing and had been on private property. I learned the hard way, mind you, that one can get a DUI for a lot of things besides driving impaired on a public road.

I fought with my board for five years, trying to get my career back, to no avail. During this time, I started another company and spent most of my time traveling around the country trying to get it off the ground. I appeared on two national shopping networks several times to sell my products. Then one day my life changed.

I had been in New York City for a week, working on my new skincare business. My last meeting in the city ran late, and I anxiously waited for Uber to take me to the airport. It was a Friday afternoon, and traffic, while never good in New York City, was extra fierce. We inched our way to LaGuardia as I anxiously checked my watch. We ended up about a quarter mile from the airport when I knew I would miss my plane.

I approached the Delta counter with trepidation, not knowing if I could get out that night to return to Seattle. I had a first-class ticket through American Express, so I hoped for the best. In the end, I was able to get out a few hours later, but would have to change planes. This was a sacrifice I was willing to make if it meant I could sleep in my own bed.

Chapter 5

Escape from New York

The first leg of the trip was uneventful, and I enjoyed the food and wine with a sunset view as we headed west. I changed planes in Minneapolis and took my seat in 3D. People filed into the plane, and I wondered who would sit next to me. I decided to close my eyes and see if I could get some sleep. Before too long, the arrival of my seatmate awakened me. I looked up and saw one of the most beautiful men I had ever laid eyes on. He smiled at me, and I melted. He had bedroom eyes and broad shoulders. I was instantly smitten.

"Hi. I'm Jacob," he said as he sat down.

"Hi. I'm Liz," I replied with a big smile.

The flight attendant brought us a glass of wine, and our conversation flowed for the entirety of the four-hour flight. We exchanged business cards and parted ways after landing. The next day, I received a text from Jacob,

So great to meet you. Are you free for coffee?

My knees were weak as I answered that I would love to get together.

Our first coffee date resulted in a four-year relationship, culminating in an engagement filled with world travel and lots of drama. Jacob and I were together for most of my problems in my medical career after the DUI, and it put a strain on our relationship. While living through the trauma and drama with the medical board, I found what I thought were PTSD symptoms returning and disrupting my daily life. My sleep was fitful, and I could feel myself retreating more and more into darkness and despair.

My days were filled with overwhelming stress and difficulties. I searched for anything that could help, but few solutions appeared. Supplements, meditation, medication, counseling, and more did very little to stop the speeding train in my mind that I was sure was about to explode into a million pieces. I did not know how I could go on in my present state. My world was closing in around me, and all I could think about was how to end my suffering.

Near the end, Jacob asked if I realized that I had broken up with him seventeen times during that same four-year period. My modus operandi was to impulsively end a stressful interpersonal situation by throwing the baby out with the proverbial bathwater. I hadn't counted the breakups, but he and I agreed to work on this relationship, as we both had real love for each other.

Over time, the pain in my life became too great to bear. As I wasn't completely suicidal again yet, I decided to travel for a while to see if I could get my head straight and calm down a bit. I had a business in Seattle that could run without me, and the freedom to do what I felt I needed to do to get healthier. I had more energy than I knew what to do with, and my mind was clouded by uncontrollable, racing thoughts. I felt like I was amped up 24/7. It was not a good feeling, but that didn't deter me from trying to start a new life for myself.

In the months prior to my first visit to Los Angeles, the wheels of my life began to come off in rapid fashion. I needed very little sleep and was overcome by hypercreativity and infinite energy. I was mostly pleasant, but occasionally, my agitation would slip into irritation and a powder keg of emotions and intense moods. I sold the estate where I raised my children and moved into a smaller home with my significant other of four years.

At first, Jacob marveled at my imagination and expansive thoughts. But over time, he became alarmed and somewhat terrified. After the move to my new home, it didn't take long for him to break up with me and move out, leaving me all alone in a new house and new city. I soon realized how much stability he had provided, and once he was gone, my life really began to unravel.

Chapter 6
The Haunted House

My youngest child departed for college in 2017, so I decided it was time to downsize. I moved from a massive house with a pool on an acre of land in one of the wealthiest suburbs of Seattle. My newly built house, although brand new, did not feel right to me. I bought it only because I was desperate to find another home, as my estate had been quickly sold. I picked the new home because it was close to my company—I would have a two-minute commute—nothing else.

Beginning the day I moved in, things were not right for me in this home. I honestly believed it was filled with evil spirits that were there to wreak havoc on my life. At that time, I had a tiny dog, and I believed she even felt the spirits and would bark incessantly at the air. I heard voices, felt the spirit's presence, and truly believed my home was haunted.

I tried the best I could to maintain any semblance of a normal life as I was falling apart by the day. I decided to become a vegan and spent hours each day shopping for and preparing exotic foods that I truly believed would change my life and help quiet my mind. During this period, I was exceptionally creative and registered over one hundred websites; created and registered innumerable trademarks; and began working on my fourth patent. 3M sticky notes were my constant friend, and when my fiancé moved out, the main floor of the house was covered in Post-its in all sizes and colors. My environment, like my mind, was a disheveled mess. This was very out of character for me as a Virgo and a former physician.

As time marched on, I became more delusional with vivid hallucinations. I became convinced that I possessed special abilities and insight. Everything in my life held a special purpose, or I rapidly disposed of it. Possessions, relationships, long-held beliefs, and my own self-identity became detached and ephemeral. I felt simultaneously alone in the real world but welcomed with open arms in my imaginary world.

With each passing day, I slipped deeper and deeper into both what would later be described as mania and a familiar depression. I knew I needed help, but did not ask for it. I thought I could steel my way through this period in my life. I was strong, having survived innumerable setbacks in my life. I was impenetrable, or so I thought.

Chapter 7

The Meeting

In the spring of 2018, after Jacob moved out, I began to lose contact with reality. The suicides of two of my heroes—Anthony Bourdain and Kate Spade—really set me back emotionally. I felt an untenable combination of anxiety and doom that kept me glued to all coincidences and conspiracy theories. I searched daily for any meaning to my life and reason to continue to live.

My new home I had just moved into, had three televisions throughout the house, and after Jacob moved out, I always kept the three on. It was comforting to have the sound of the shows to keep me company. Walking from room to room, I watched a custom and curated selection of television shows that became increasingly bizarre, which I believed were targeted at me. I was convinced that my television shows were being curated by Steve Jobs for my sole benefit, and he often appeared on the television screen to talk with me and give me directions. He and I could literally communicate through the television.

During this time, about three months long, I was told by Steve through the television that I would get gastrointestinal cancer, just like him, if I didn't slow down and change my lifestyle, high stress filled with disappointment and rage, just like his life (he let me know.)

Another major message from Steve through the television regarded suicidal celebrities. Kendrick Lamar and Khloe Kardashian were both reported to me by Steve to be at the end of their rope and in need of urgent intervention, thus leading me to visit California in an attempt to save them. I believed I had been tasked to help them through their crises by the Divine and Steve Jobs. One thing's for sure: I was the one having the crisis, but I clearly didn't know it at the time.

As the wheels were coming off my life, I recruited comrades to join me in my new business ventures that I planned on exploring on my visits to Los Angeles. I had limitless energy and ideas.

On impulse, I reached out to an acquaintance who had set up the website and app for one of the world's biggest companies. I believed him to be the perfect person to launch my ideas digitally, as I had big plans for myself. Prior to going to California, the businessman had come to my hometown from New York City to meet with me and work out the details of our association. It just so happened that he was available and interested in my project. We decided to pursue my ideas further with an in-person meeting in Seattle.

I flew the businessman out first class to Seattle from New York City. He offered to take an Uber to my home, where I was hosting him, but I chose to pick him up at the airport myself.

It was a clear and crisp evening as I headed to the airport. I put the top down on my SL550 and enjoyed the ride with the wind in my hair, blaring my favorite music, Coldplay and Taylor Swift. I arrived at the airport before he landed and waited with schoolgirl anticipation. I had never met him before in person and only had a FaceTime meeting from years ago to identify him. I searched the curb outside the airport and saw him. *OMG.* He was tall, chiseled, and suntanned. He was bearded with longish hair and piercing blue eyes. Holy shit. He was Adonis.

He walked confidently toward the car, and I waved at him out of the open top.

"Hi, Mark!" I shouted at him.

He smiled broadly and approached the passenger side of the car. "Wow, you don't look sixty-five!" he said with a look of surprise.

"Sixty-five?" I asked.

"You told me you were sixty-five!" he said.

I thought for a moment, *What the hell is he talking about? I wasn't close to being sixty-five and still got carded!* The only sixty-five I was aware of was my birth year.

"I was born in sixty-five," I stated.

"Ooooohhh, I see," he said in a long, slow voice, but then didn't say anything else.

"What year were you born in?" I finally asked to break the silence.

"Nineteen sixty-five," he said.

Interesting, I thought, and pulled the convertible out into traffic.

The purpose of this trip was to decide if we would work together and iron out the details of our association if we chose to proceed. The chemistry was palpable between us, our goals aligned quickly, and he agreed to join my team. The visit was short, just long enough to plan our future, and he flew back to the East Coast far too soon. I could have talked with him forever, it seemed. He was so worldly and smart, my kind of guy. We clicked and made plans to travel together to Los Angeles soon to pursue my new business.

Chapter 8
911

Before I decided it was time to visit California, I had a few more episodes in my new home that further confirmed my need to get out and sell it. One evening, all alone with my dog, I believed the world was coming to an end. I felt trapped, like a caged animal, and I felt like I was going to die. I did not feel safe driving myself to the hospital, so I called 911. What ensued is hard for me to put together, even with 20/20 hindsight.

After I dialed 911, I was put on hold for what seemed like a long time. "911, what is your emergency?" a lady finally asked.

"I think I'm dying," I replied.

"You've called the city. You need the county emergency services," she said. "Hold please."

I waited for about ten minutes on hold, while hyperventilating, and then another person answered. "911, what is your emergency?" a second woman asked.

"I think I am dying," I replied.

"You need the city, not the county emergency services. Hold while I transfer you," she finished.

I was transferred back to the city and remained on hold—for an emergency, mind you—for over fifteen additional minutes until I hung up. I decided to go to bed and see if I could wake up to a better situation. I lay in bed, and my little dog began barking at the air again. I put her on the floor next to the bed, and she ran downstairs. I was too tired to follow her, so I decided to just go to sleep.

A while later—I'm not sure how long—I was awakened by a deafening clap of thunder and lightning. I opened my eyes and saw a bolt of lightning come through my ceiling and down onto my duvet cover. I screamed and jumped out of bed. My ears were ringing from the force of the sound, and I felt off-balance. In the distance, I heard my dog barking from downstairs. I decided to go down and check things out.

As I walked down the stairs, I could hear the dog's bark getting louder, but it didn't sound like she was indoors. The last time I had seen her was upstairs, and the house was completely shut up and locked. I walked through the kitchen to the patio door and noticed my dog— outside the locked door—barking at me to let her in.

"How the hell did you get out there?" I asked her under my breath as I let her in.

There was truly no way to explain how she got outside. At this point, I knew I couldn't stay in this house any longer. The next day, I tore apart my beautiful new home. I was anxious and paranoid. I stopped going to my office because I couldn't keep it together anymore. I was too agitated to focus on anything, so I spent my days working on new creative projects and planning my escape from my hometown, which was filled with so much grief and misery. I had saved over $100,000 cash in the prior decade and packed it and prepared for my departure.

Chapter 9

Heading to California

I decided to visit Southern California. I figured I could work on my new business idea there, and I certainly could use some sunshine, having lived in a cold, dark, rainy climate most of my life.

Going to California, in hindsight, was a mistake. When I left for my first visit to Los Angeles, I was rarely in touch with reality. In my altered state of mind, I conceived of a massive company that incorporated media, entertainment, consumer products, and charitable services that would further push me into the global, successful business world.

In all my infinite wisdom, I decided to charter a jet to Los Angeles. I brought my new colleague, Mark, for my start-up and, of course, my masseuse, Bob. Why wouldn't I bring my masseuse? It all seemed so logical. I flew Mark out from New York City to join me for the private jet ride from Seattle to Los Angeles.

The day of the flight was a gorgeous summer day with clear skies and light winds. Waiting in the private aviation lounge for our jet to be ready, I was buoyed by a sense of excitement and optimism. Doubt and fear were nowhere to be seen. It was a glorious day.

We three walked out on the tarmac toward our awaiting jet. The wind was fierce as we approached the plane with the familiar screech of the high-performance engine typical of a Learjet. As a physician, I had been an aviation medical examiner. I loved pilots and flight of all kinds: planes, helicopters, and spaceships. I grabbed my masseuse by the arm and twirled us both in a circle as I filmed the three-sixty-degree Selfie, ready to post on social media, of course.

Stepping on the jet was like entering another world. The bar was fully stocked, champagne glasses waiting, cool music playing. We took our seats throughout the plane—initially spreading out—but quickly returning to a joyous huddle near the bar. Our two pilots were fantastic, and we took an endless stream of pictures as we soared above the terrain on our way to Los Angeles.

As the private jet approached our destination, my feeling of euphoria elevated even more. We landed at Burbank Airport and hung out on the tarmac after landing for a while to celebrate our arrival.

It was a near-perfect day: clear, cloudless skies with a gentle breeze. We took lots of photos together in front of the plane, and Mark put his arm around me tightly for one photo and joked about us being on the cover of *TIME* magazine one day. Life seemed so hopeful again.

Chapter 10
Advent in Los Angeles

After I paid the $8,000 bill for the ride, we eventually hopped into an Uber to head downtown. To be honest, I didn't think about the fact that I could have flown all three of us to Los Angeles first class for a fraction of the cost. My mind was preoccupied by expanding my life in any way I could.

The air of excitement in the car was palpable. We drove into town and headed toward the Beverly Hills Resort. I chose this hotel because I had stayed there previously and absolutely loved it. It is a lavish, old-world hotel with suites surrounding a mid-century modern pool area. It was, without a doubt, a place to see and be seen.

I shared a suite with my masseuse, and the businessman had his own suite. Every suite came with a formal dining room and an area to entertain. Each night, we would meet to unwind and have dinner together and discuss business, in addition to our daytime meetings. I had hired away the businessman from one of America's most admired companies, owned by one of the world's richest men. I had met Mark six years previously through another work contact at Starbucks. He is an app and website developer, and I engaged him to develop both of those for my new company. It was a bit uncomfortable knowing his recent boss was upset that I had lured him away from his company, but I tried not to let it bother me too much, but it was always on my mind.

One night after dinner, I decided to leave my suite to roam around the hotel property. I was antsy and agitated. My meetings weren't going as planned, and I was getting tired of the masseuse. I put on my headphones and played my favorite music at a high volume. I lit a cigarette and headed downstairs to the pool. Once there, I had the brilliant idea to go take a dip in the pool while fully clothed, with a cigarette in hand. Unfortunately, and due to my mental state at the time, I dove into the water with my phone in hand and earbuds in my ears. I came up out of the water and started to laugh hysterically. Why I thought that was funny is still a puzzle to me.

I exited the water, cigarette still in hand, and headed back up to my suite, dripping wet. On the way, I noticed a staircase leading to the roof of the hotel. I decided to take advantage of the opportunity to dance and sing at the top of my lungs on the roof. As you might imagine, I garnered some attention at that point.

My son, Michael, had come over for dinner that night and was still in my suite when I decided to dance at elevation. He came out of my suite and instructed me to get off the roof. I not-so-politely declined and continued to dance and sing. Michael climbed up on the roof himself and eventually convinced me to come down, but not before we got into a huge screaming fight. This episode was a nail in the coffin of our relationship, which had deteriorated significantly in the short time since I had arrived in Los Angeles, his hometown.

After a few more days of meetings where I endeavored to keep it together, Mark and my masseuse returned to their respective homes. Over the next several months, Mark and I met a few more times when we both traveled to California, but my project was slow to get off the ground. After a few months of working together, I terminated our association as I believed he was not putting in a serious effort to my project. Additionally, I was concerned he was using my expertise to help his former boss compete with my ideas.

Chapter 11

Buying the Car

I knew when I arrived in California that I was there to help Khloe and Kendrick. I just didn't know when or how. After the men left, I switched hotels and left Beverly Hills for the Valley, where I knew the celebrities lived that I had been called to save. The first thing I needed to do was get wheels. I knew exactly what I wanted: a white G550 Mercedes G-wagon. Of course, it sounded reasonable to purchase a car of this caliber for a *visit* to Los Angeles to add to my other two white Mercedes at home. It was completely logical in my mind.

In true California fashion, I dressed to the nines to shop for a car. That day, I wore tight black jeans, black UGGs (even though it was August in California,) a black cami, and a black leather jacket. Of course, the Submariner Rolex, Birkin bag, and diamonds joined the look. I had to say that I didn't feel that I looked my age of fifty-two, especially since I kept getting carded. I think it was the lack of sun damage because I didn't come from a sunny locale. Where I lived was known for its poor weather, another draw to visit California.

That beautiful day in California made me feel like I had something to celebrate, and I could barely contain my ear-to-ear smile from the pleasure of seeing the sun. I grabbed my Chanel sunglasses and left my hotel to get a new car.

I took an Uber from the Four Seasons in the Valley down the 101 to Calabasas Mercedes. I eagerly jumped out of the car and walked directly over to a white G-Wagon. I scanned the exterior long enough to have a sales associate come to my aid and let me into the car.

"Hi. My name is Heather. Would you like to take the vehicle for a test drive?"

"Yes, absolutely," I replied.

She fetched the keys from inside the dealership, and away we went. It took me five minutes to fall in love with my dream car and say yes, so we quickly returned to the dealership to write up the purchase. I looked at the price, $150,000, and didn't blink an eye. I bought the car with a down payment, and soon I was ready to get on with my mission.

"What do you have planned for the rest of your day, Liz?" Heather asked.

"I'm going to Malibu," I said.

"Do you have big plans?" she asked again.

"Actually, I've never been. I want to have dinner at Nobu and see the sun set over the Pacific."

"Beautiful place. Here you go!" she said as she handed me the keys.

I thanked her and walked out to my new car, one that cost more than many people's mortgages. *Thank you, God, for letting me experience this beautiful vehicle*, I thought as I started the engine.

I patted the console of the car and said out loud, "Let's go to Nobu Malibu!"

Chapter 12
Nobu Malibu

I stopped by the hotel and changed my clothes into something more suitable for a fancy dinner. I set the GPS to Nobu, and it showed me that I would have to go to the 101 and down Malibu Canyon Road to get there. It was my first time on that road, and the cliffs were fierce and amazing. The drive to Nobu was uneventful, but terrifying. In the setting sun dusk, the decline in elevation was remarkable, and the road was narrow.

Many people don't know that Malibu is massive, spanning twenty-one miles of prime Southern California (SoCal) coastline. Malibu is further informally divided into the public/southern area and the intensely private/northern area, where celebrities and non-celebrities commune casually. Nobu resides at the intersection of the public and private Malibu, attracting throngs of celebrities, titans of business, locals, and gawkers. The awesome thing about Nobu is that all celebrities are left alone and very protected by the staff.

The night I arrived at Nobu, Kendall Jenner was there with throngs of friends, yet you would hardly know she was even there because she was so protected by the staff. I had only heard of the legendary restaurant and couldn't wait to eat there, although I would have preferred to have company.

By the time I made it to Malibu, the sun was setting, and darkness was on its way, but it wasn't too dark to see the packed parking lot filled with exotic cars that dwarfed my G-Wag. I thought to myself, *Holy sheesh!* This was real money, and it smelled like real money. As I pulled into the packed parking lot, I swapped my flip-flops (a legitimate shoe in California) for my four-inch strappy sandals.

I pulled up to the gorgeous bellhop and waited for him to open my door. "Have a reservation with us tonight, miss?" he asked.

I was amused at the "miss" reference and quickly let him know I didn't have reservations. "I'm headed to the bar," I said.

"Wonderful," he said, and instructed me to leave the car on.

I hadn't known what to wear to dinner at Nobu, but I assumed the casual chic atmosphere in SoCal would serve me well. I wore white jeans, strappy silver sandals, and a coral, silk, flowy top. A vintage Louis Vuitton purse, a gold presidential Rolex, and pearls completed the look.

When I arrived, throngs of people were standing outside the restaurant waiting to get in. I quickly surveyed the scene and noted the usual in California, people dressed to the nines, all the way to jeans and a T-shirt. I fit right in.

The attendant opened my door, and I proceeded to fall out of the car. My heel got caught on the running board, and I slipped down the side of the car, landing on the ground. Unfortunately, simultaneous to my fall from the car were ten or so flashes of the cameras of the paparazzi, who I hadn't noticed standing on the sidewalk outside the restaurant along Pacific Coast Highway (PCH).

Mortified, I picked myself up off the ground with the help of the attendant. "Now what do I do?" I asked him, referencing the cameras and thinking of what a sight that must have been.

He smiled sweetly at me. "Don't worry. I'll make sure nothing gets out to the tabloids."

I was amused at the thought until I saw him motion to the cameramen I was not a person worthy of photographing. *Ouch. Oh well! Off to dinner at one of the world's iconic restaurants,* I thought to myself.

I exited the parking lot and headed toward the restaurant. I hadn't been visiting California long enough to get used to the stares from people around me. It's a national pastime in Los Angeles, with everyone hoping to see a celebrity. Although I was anything but a celebrity, I had enough bling and dressed like someone who belonged there, so I got the stares.

I walked up to the outside seating area of Nobu and saw the only seat available, snuggled between an Asian party and an older man with a gaggle of beautiful young women around him. As I approached his table, the only one with a free seat, the handsome older man gestured for me to sit with them, next to him on the couch. Given that I didn't see any choice, I gratefully took the seat and introduced myself to the group.

The man, named Sergi, was a land developer originally from Moscow, now an American. The girls were sweet and looked like they were twenty-one years old or so. It was clear why Sergi brought the women, and he appeared to want to make me one of them.

"Why don't you join us after dinner?" Sergi asked.

"What are you doing after dinner?" I asked.

"Going back to party at my mansion in Malibu," he said.

"Oh, come! It will be so fun to have you join us," one of the beautiful girls said in a heavy, Eastern European accent.

I thought about it for a minute and couldn't get my mind off the orgy I imagined would be taking place. "Next time," I said in a rare moment of lucidity.

Dinner was exquisite, and Sergi knew the menu well. He ordered for the table and wouldn't let me pay for anything: black cod, brussels sprouts, sushi, Kobe beef, and more. The menu had it all, and the food was exquisite.

Sergi interacted with the waitstaff like a familiar family. Laughing and joking with them only made the treats from the kitchen come faster. Cristal champagne flowed, and the evening seemed perfect and magical. I tried not to be rude and ignore my tablemates as I snuck a peek at the other patrons and the mighty Pacific Ocean laid out in front of me. The evening flew by, and true darkness descended after a spectacular sunset.

Sergi tried to convince me again to join them at his home after dinner, but I knew what that meant—sex, drugs, and no sleep—all of which I didn't need. I politely declined, thanked Sergi profusely for dinner, and made my way back to the G-Wag with the valet.

I approached the stand, teeming with a new crowd coming in at that late hour, and handed the young man my ticket and a twenty-dollar bill. My car was there in a flash, and I hopped in and started my way toward the area where the hotel lodging was in Malibu. What I didn't think about was the fact that it was a beautiful summer weekend night in Malibu; there were literally no available rooms.

Chapter 13
No Room at the Inn

I cruised PCH looking for a hotel room. No one had any availability, and some innkeepers thought it was amusing that I thought I could get a hotel room at ten o'clock on a Friday, August night in Malibu.

As I drove down PCH, I placed my hope on one final place to stay. I pulled into the SeaShore Motel, parked in the only available space, and entered the lobby. Behind the desk sat an impossibly handsome man, de rigueur for Malibu and Los Angeles in general.

"Hi. Do you have a room for the night?" I asked.

The man looked at me as if I had two heads and said bluntly, "We've been booked for months."

"Do you know of any other options in Malibu?"

He quickly replied, "No, but you can take that pretty little G-Wag and just sleep in it on PCH."

I looked at him rather shocked, and quickly left the lobby. Walking back to my car, I started to cry. Suddenly, I reconsidered what I was doing. I was overcome with fear, anxiety, and dread. I was all alone in a strange city without the executive functioning to know what to do next. I had completely forgotten about my hotel room in the Valley at the Four Seasons.

Chapter 14
Jerry

I slowly pulled my car out of the driveway of the SeaShore Motel and turned south onto PCH. As I did, I nearly hit a man carrying his surfboard and walking toward his van on the ocean side of the road. I thought I might have recognized him, which in hindsight was preposterous as I was new to Los Angeles, so I slowed to a crawl and rolled down my passenger window.

"Hey!" I shouted at him out the window.

He turned toward me with a big smile and said, "Hey, back at ya!"

The man wasn't wearing a shirt, and I noticed his chiseled, tanned body. He was barefoot and wearing the typical shorts of a boarder.

"I'm looking for a place to sleep tonight," I blurted out. In my present state, I had lost all inhibition.

"I know just the place. Follow me," he said confidently as he gestured toward a dilapidated Volkswagen van ahead on the right.

I slowly followed him as he approached his van and motioned for me to park in front of him. I hopped out of my car and locked it before heading to meet him at the back of his van.

"Hi. I'm Jerry," he said as he smiled and looked at me slowly and carefully from head to toe. He had a gorgeous face and big blue eyes, the color and size of the ocean. "I've been surfing all day and am about to have dinner. Care to join me?"

Dinner? At eleven o'clock at night? I thought to myself.

"I already ate, but thank you." I investigated the open rear door of the van and realized this wasn't just a car. It was potentially his home. "Do you live here?" I blurted out.

"Yes, I've been at this same spot for years." I was simultaneously horrified and intrigued. "Come on. Let's hop in," he said as he gestured to get in the van.

I looked for a place to step and found every available surface covered with surfboards, clothes, flip-flops, food, Grateful Dead memorabilia, and marijuana paraphernalia.

Jerry helped me into the van and indicated which pile of clothes I should sit on. "Care for a hit?" he asked as he proffered a bong.

"When in Rome," I replied as I inhaled from the bong.

"You can stay with me tonight," Jerry said as he exhaled his own hit.

"You mean here?" I asked, somewhat surprised.

"Yes! I've got a blanket and pillow just for you," he replied.

Wow, I thought. *What the hell am I doing? Staying with a homeless stranger on PCH? Jesus, Liz.*

But did I really have any options at this point? Of course, I had completely forgotten that I had a luxury hotel room paid for and waiting for me in the Valley. My mind was fried, and my neurons were just as crispy as I drew a blank on any other rational options.

"Sure," I said to Jerry, "I'll stay with you tonight."

We sat in silence for a while and exchanged bong hits. I tried not to stare too obviously at his home. I had never seen anything quite like it before. While I probably should have been fearful at that point, I flung caution to the wind and took a slow, deep breath, followed by a big, long sigh.

"Let's go down to the ocean," Jerry said as he loaded up another bowl.

The night sky was cloudless and full of stars. There wasn't a sound, except for the crashing of waves, as Jerry led me down a steep, dark embankment wedged between two oceanfront homes.

"Aren't we trespassing, Jerry?" I whispered as we reached the sand.

"Don't worry about it. I know everyone here," he replied as he grabbed my hand and led me to the edge of the water. "I'm the unofficial mayor of Malibu."

Once standing at the water's edge, Jerry stood next to me, holding my hand. "Liz ..." he said as he turned to me. He swung me around and into his arms. The full moon above us provided an exquisite backdrop for our first embrace. "Look at me," he said. "Where have you been all my life?"

At that moment, a huge sneaker wave crashed at our feet. I screamed with surprise and started to run away from the sea. Jerry joined me and practically lifted me off the ground as we chased the dry sand.

"Let's go up here," Jerry said as he gestured toward a sheltered area under one of the houses built on stilts, looming above us. Jerry led the way to a flat, sandy area and produced a blanket seemingly out of nowhere. He sat down on the blanket and held his outstretched hand to me. "Here, have a seat with me."

I complied, and Jerry wrapped me in his strong arms. "Good night, love of my life," he said as he laid me down next to his body.

"Good night, Jerry," I said in a soft voice. "Really nice to meet you."

Chapter 15
The Adventures with Jerry Begin

I woke up the next morning, and Jerry was gone. I had sand in my hair and my clothes, and I struggled to make sense of where I was. I slowly got to my feet and dragged the blanket up the hill to where my car was next to Jerry's van. My car seemed fine, so I walked to Jerry's van. A handmade sign was posted on the passenger's front window that read "Gone Surfing."

I walked around the van and knocked on the windows. "Jerry?" I called as I peeked in the dirty windows. I soon realized he really was gone and headed back to my car.

I opened my car door and sat down behind the wheel. Malibu was just starting to come to life, and my headache was telling me it was time for coffee. I started the car and turned on the air-conditioning and my favorite music. I searched my phone for a coffee place but came up empty-handed as my new phone didn't get good reception in Malibu. As I began to inch forward south on PCH, I saw Jerry running toward me, carrying two cups of coffee.

"Liz!" he shouted at me.

I stopped the car and rolled down the window. "Hey, Jerry. I thought I lost you."

"Liz, you can always find me here," Jerry said as he reached inside my open car window and unlocked the door to let himself in. "Here, I got you a coffee." He handed it to me. "Organic coffee with organic almond milk."

That's pretty fancy for a homeless guy, I thought but was grateful for the caffeine.

"That was very sweet of you," I responded. Little did I know that that would be the last time he purchased anything for me, or us.

"I see you got the Malibu Barbie/soccer mom car," Jerry said as he smiled and patted the dashboard of the G-Wag. "Do a U-turn now and head north on PCH. I want to take you to breakfast."

I dutifully complied, and we drove north in silence for a while past Pepperdine University. I could feel Jerry staring at me, and I occasionally glanced at him and smiled if our eyes met. He was impossibly handsome, sun-kissed with shaggy, sun-bleached hair and a trim, brown beard. He was the perfect picture of a California surfer dude, and I was excited at the thought of hanging out with him.

Chapter 16
Breakfast at Malibu Diner

It seemed like I was driving a long way, so I broke the silence and, feeling like a child on a car trip with their parents, asked, "Are we almost there?"

"Yes, take a left at the next light," he replied. "I'm taking you to the Malibu Diner, the best breakfast in Malibu."

I parked the car, and we entered a tiny restaurant in a strip mall.

"Jerry!" a short, round lady exclaimed as she ran to him with outstretched arms. "You devil! Where have you been?"

They held each other in an embrace. After a long hug, they chatted to each other for what seemed like too much time.

Jerry finally turned to me and said, "This is my friend, Anna. She owns this place."

Anna smiled, waved at me, and motioned us to a two-top near the window. Jerry and I ordered the same thing: a machaca breakfast burrito and another cup of coffee. We kept the small talk flowing along with the coffee refills, and soon, we were planning our next adventure.

Anna brought us our check and tried handing it to Jerry. He motioned for her to give it to me and said, "Liz, you don't mind getting this, do you? I'm a little low on cash right now."

Although I was surprised at being asked to pay after he had said he was taking *me* to breakfast, I didn't let on that I was anything but cool with it. "No problem, Jerry," I replied as I handed her $40 cash.

Jerry was the ideal accomplice for me at that time: a drifter, a surfer, a con man, and an iconoclast, the perfect backdrop to my former life filled with rules, obligations, responsibilities, and pressure. He was crazy, really, and so was I at that time. We were a combustible combination and wasted no time getting into trouble.

What ensued over the next few weeks was a life I had only read about in the tabloids. Our days were spent dreaming and plotting our future together, dreaming big and throwing caution to the wind. I loved the excitement of it all and truly believed Jerry and I were going to make it big in the land of opportunity.

Jerry was a man of champagne tastes and caviar dreams. If only he had had even a beer budget to go with it, things might have been different, perhaps better. But I soon learned that Jerry was a man of extraordinary debt and prior arrests. He had spent significant stints of time in jail in between living in various vehicles on PCH and surfing, and his life was in shambles. Estranged from a future former wife and two children, he had been a very successful professional earlier in life and held a master's degree. He was a man of extremes, and I was a woman of extremes (at that time in my life).

Jerry's modus operandi was to simultaneously build me up when he wanted me to pay for something and tear me down at most other times. I saw him simultaneously as my SoCal guide and my tormentor. After we met on PCH that summer night, we were pretty much inseparable for the next few months.

Whenever I was in Los Angeles, we split our time between his VW parked on the streets of Malibu and the luxury hotels I paid for throughout Los Angeles, the Northern Valley, and Malibu. He drove the G-Wag like he owned it, despite not even having a valid driver's license. He liked the upper-crust life, and I liked the companionship. It was, as they say, a match made in hell.

Jerry was very familiar with Los Angeles, and Malibu in particular, and he was a good tour guide for me. After breakfast, we hopped back into the car with Jerry driving this time. He took us off PCH and drove up into the mountains of Malibu. I was taken aback by the incredible beauty of the area—rugged cliffs diving down to the Pacific Ocean, expansive views, cloudless blue skies, gentle breezes swaying the palm trees, and the two of us. It was incredibly romantic and exciting to me, especially after being dumped by my fiancé.

After a couple hours of exploring, Jerry decided it was time to move on. "Hey, Liz, where are you staying?"

"I'm in the Valley at the Four Seasons," I replied, having finally remembered.

"Let's go there! I love the Four Seasons." Given where I had met him—homeless in Malibu—I wondered when he had ever been to that hotel or chain. "I need to stop by my van and get some things before we go," he continued. After sleeping on the beach, I was excited at the prospect of staying with Jerry in a luxury hotel.

We inched our way back to Malibu in fierce traffic and stopped by Jerry's van. He hopped out of the car while double-parking on PCH. When he received horn honks for doing so, Jerry smiled and waved at the angry motorists.

He really does think he owns this town, I said to myself.

Jerry returned to the driver's seat with an armload of items.

"Don't you need to move your van, Jerry?" I asked.

"No, they won't touch it. The cops know it's my van," he replied.

I had seen a lot of other cars/vans/RVs parked on the side of PCH in Malibu, so I figured he knew what he was talking about.

Chapter 17
Shopping Spree

We drove from Malibu back to the Valley. As we approached the hotel, Jerry suddenly had a stroke of genius and said, "Hey, Liz, I really could use some new clothes. Can we go shopping?"

Based on the non-payment for breakfast, I surmised that Jerry needed money to procure these clothes as well. "Sure, Jerry, let's go shopping. I could use some clothes, too."

Jerry drove us to the nearest mall, and we entered the clothing store, arm in arm.

"We're here!" Jerry exclaimed to no one in particular as we entered the store with a spring in our step.

"Welcome to Ross," the uniformed guard at the door said in reply.

It didn't take long before Jerry and I had filled two shopping carts with clothes, shoes, accessories, and housewares. To be honest, it was the most fun I've ever had shopping, as I usually hate to shop. Jerry ran his cart around the store like an ill-behaved child, and we spent a lot of time dressing each other in various outfits and talking about all the places we would wear the clothes. I had been steadily losing weight over the past year (without trying), and I finally enjoyed shopping with Jerry for new clothes with my new figure.

We pulled up our carts to check out, and the clerk asked if we had found everything. Jerry replied, "I could go get more!"

I interjected, "I think we've done enough damage for today, Jerry." I felt like a parent with one of my sons.

Our total at Ross was over $3,000, but I was unconcerned about it. I had big plans for my future and believed this was just a drop in the proverbial bucket. Jerry changed his clothes in the car, replacing his shorts and frayed T-shirt with a pair of chinos, a polo shirt, and canvas shoes. We loaded up the car with our spoils and headed to the hotel. The bellhop greeted us with a cart and helped us to my room.

The hotel was stunning and fit for a queen. It's hard to describe the understated elegance of the Four Seasons chain, and I felt that I fit right in. Jerry, with his new clothes, seemed to fit in, too.

Once in our room, we walked around the vast, elegant suite and marveled at the opulence. Jerry's first job was to take a shower, and I was glad he did. Homeless in a car on PCH doesn't come with very good amenities, that's for sure. Jerry came out of the bathroom, and with a towel still around his waist, he proceeded to unplug all the electronics in the suite and put a towel over all three televisions. He was convinced we were being spied on and the government was tracking him through video surveillance via our electronics. This was my first exposure to someone almost as paranoid as I was at that time, and it made me edgier. I did not need any help in feeling suspicious.

Jerry and I spent a few days at the hotel, thoroughly enjoying ourselves, eating, drinking, sitting by the pool, and going to the Four Seasons spa. But after a couple of days, Jerry's mood became labile, and he told me he needed to get back to his van in Malibu. I sensed that he needed to be in the ocean, and the Valley was very far away from it, as compared to his van.

We packed up his clothes and headed back to Malibu. Once there, I drove to the spot where we had left his van, but the van was gone.

"What the fuck happened to my vehicle? Where the hell are my surfboards?" Jerry exclaimed as he surveyed the scene where he used to live. "Dammit! Now I must pay to get it out of hock … again!"

"This has happened before?" I asked, genuinely surprised.

"Yes, a few times," he replied honestly. "Can I count on you, Liz, to help me out here?"

I felt trapped, but I hoped we could continue our time together. "Sure, Jerry, I'll help you out."

Jerry knew exactly where to go to pick up his van and drove us straight there. We approached what looked like a used car lot, and Jerry spotted it right away.

"How much is this going to cost?" I asked Jerry.

"I'll let you know after I find out," he replied.

He jumped out of the car and disappeared for about ten minutes. When he returned, he handed me a piece of paper showing the handwritten total amount due, $2,100. I dug into my purse, counted out the money, and handed it to Jerry.

"Thanks, Liz. I owe you one," he said as he took the money.

You certainly do, I thought to myself.

Jerry wanted to take his van back to "his" spot on PCH, and I really didn't want to stay in Malibu at that moment, so we parted ways at the towing company. Jerry didn't have a phone, so if I wanted to see him, I would need to drive to Malibu. I didn't know when I would see him again, which really bummed me out because he was the first anchor I had in SoCal. We said goodbye with a long embrace.

"I really dig you, Liz," Jerry said as he hugged me tightly.

"I dig you, too, Jerry," I replied.

Chapter 18

Four Seasons

I drove back to the Four Seasons and parked my car with the valet. After I got out of the car, I decided to hang out with the bellhops for a while, killing some time. I heard one of them say to another, "Mimi will be arriving soon."

"Who's Mimi?" I asked.

"She's one of our residents here. She's a VIP," a bellhop replied.

A few minutes later, a woman drove up to the entrance in my dream car, a white convertible Aston Martin with a cream leather interior. I not only loved this car, but I had even named one of my companies after it.

I decided I had nothing to lose. As Mimi got out of her car, I approached her, introduced myself, and handed her one of my business cards. I told her how much I loved her car, and she looked at me and smiled. She was breathtakingly beautiful and probably about ten years older than I was.

"Here, take it for a spin," she said as she tossed me her keys.

I looked at the bellhop with a quizzical look, to which he said, "Take it! She's serious."

As she walked into the Four Seasons Hotel, her home, I got behind the wheel and sat for a few minutes.

A bellhop came to the car and said, "So are you going to take it for a drive?"

I gave it a second thought and replied, "No, I'll just pull it over there for you guys."

The car looked, felt, and smelled like success and money. *One day*, I thought to myself.

After I parked the Aston Martin, I went back to my suite and had a cigarette on the balcony overlooking the pool. I had no idea how I was going to build a new company in a new city the likes of Los Angeles, but I was sure I was on the precipice of massive success.

I decided to order room service and then go to the spa and indoor pool. As I waited for my dinner to arrive, I hopped on my computer and surfed the internet. Steve Jobs was waiting for me and proceeded to show me my future: reality television show (starring Jerry and me, obviously), consumer products business, fashion brand, charitable foundation, and so forth. I was comforted knowing there was a master plan for me and didn't think to question the veracity of what I was seeing. It was completely 100% real in my mind.

Dinner arrived quickly, and I marveled at the spread: New York strip steak grilled to perfection, roasted asparagus, Caesar salad, and a glass of Sterling Cabernet. Life seemed nearly perfect at that moment, and I was optimistic about my future.

After dinner, I put on my swimsuit and headed to the spa. I was alone in the vast, indoor pool and jacuzzi until an older woman came in and sat close enough to me to have a conversation. She introduced herself and indicated she was also a permanent resident of the hotel, just like Mimi. I was fascinated to learn what life was like living in such a situation and even considered it for myself, should I move to Los Angeles.

We continued to chat as we both swam and took a jacuzzi. After a while, I let her know I had to go to bed, and she asked if we could keep in touch. I told her I would drop a business card at the front desk for her, but never did.

Chapter 19
Malibu Living

I left Los Angeles for Seattle and worked on my business there for a few weeks, but I missed California and Jerry every day. I decided it was time to go back, so I booked a commercial ticket and arrived in Los Angeles without being able to get in touch with Jerry. Once I landed, I drove to Malibu and searched for Jerry's van. I found it in a different place along PCH. He wasn't there, so I headed to the water to see if he was surfing. He was.

I sat on the sand and watched Jerry surf for a while. He had previously been a world champion in surfing, and it was incredible to watch him navigate the SoCal waves with precision and aplomb. I had previously taken a surfing lesson from one of his friends, and it was a humiliating and embarrassing experience. I was not born with the snowboard/skateboard/surfboard gene, and gave up trying to surf after several unsuccessful hours. But Jerry was a pro, and he knew it. It only added to his allure and arrogance.

Jerry finally had enough of surfing and walked toward me on the beach. "Liz!" he shouted at me. "I didn't know you were coming back!"

I got up from the sand, and Jerry gave me a bear hug. He smelled like the sea and covered me with water, but I didn't care. I was so happy to be back in California with him.

"Jerry, I need to get a hotel. Do you want to stay with me?" I asked.

"Yes!" he replied. "I know just the place. There is a great place at the north end of Malibu. Let me get my stuff from the van, and we can go now."

Staying in Malibu would mean I was a long way from my planned business meetings and reserved hotel room in Los Angeles, but at that moment, I didn't care.

We walked back to his van, and Jerry immediately lit a bong while standing on the sidewalk. Tourists walked by, and Jerry engaged them and offered bong hits to anyone who would partake. It seemed that Jerry was a bit more unroofed than the last time I saw him, but I threw caution to the wind and continued with our day's plans. Jerry packed up a few items in a paper bag, and we hopped into my car and headed north with Jerry behind the wheel of the G-Wag.

Chapter 20
Malibu Retreat

We drove the fifteen-plus-mile trip to the northernmost part of Malibu and turned into the entrance of Malibu Retreat, a sweet, mid-century motel with charm galore. Jerry checked us in, pretty much ignoring me, making it seem he was the big man on campus until it came time to pay. I handed the clerk my Platinum American Express card, and we were led to our room. Once there, Jerry and I looked at each other and said in unison, "Now what?"

Without much thought, we decided it was time to look for houses to live in. We grabbed a few Malibu magazines from the motel lobby and began our search. After about an hour, we had created an itinerary and set out to find our next crib.

Jerry drove us up again into the hills of Malibu. Even with being safely inside my car, built like a tank, the drive was terrifying. Steep roads had hairpin turns around deep ravines and cliffs. Jerry drove like we were on a racetrack, and I was sure we were going to meet our demise, but I didn't let on that I was freaking out inside.

We spent several hours driving to numerous mansions for sale and were even allowed inside by a couple of homeowners. Although the houses were listed for millions of dollars, I didn't blink an eye and envisioned myself making an offer on one of them. I imagined a home where I could pursue my next business venture and Jerry could surf whenever he wished.

We finished our day of shopping for a home with a stop at a rare dive bar in Malibu and had a beer and nachos.

Back at the motel, Jerry let me know he was very tired from surfing and needed to go to bed. I took the towel off the television put there by Jerry and watched a few shows before trying to fall asleep myself. After a couple of hours of tossing and turning, I got out of bed and went to my car. I turned on some music and rested my head against the headrest.

Suddenly, a wave of fear and terror wafted over me, and I had a vision of being kidnapped from my car by armed robbers. My phone didn't get a signal in northern Malibu, so I was unable to call anyone for help, and it didn't occur to me to go inside and talk with Jerry. I felt paralyzed in my seat with fear. I knew I needed help, so I decided to call the Mercedes emergency line.

I pressed the red button on the ceiling of my car and waited.

"Mercedes-Benz, what is your emergency?" a nice voice asked through the car's sound system.

"Hi. I'm sitting in my car, and I believe I am in serious danger," I replied.

"I can help," she answered. "I will need your vehicle identification number (VIN), please."

I searched my glove compartment for any identifying information without luck. "I don't see a VIN."

"Look on your windshield," she stated.

I struggled in the dark to read the tiny letters and numbers and wasn't sure what a VIN had to do with anything anyway. I read the VIN to the lady several times, and she let me know that Mercedes didn't have my VIN on file. I was speechless and didn't know what to do.

At that moment, about one o'clock in the morning, a text message came through on my phone despite the terrible reception from my son, asking if I was okay.

Mom, where are you? Are you okay? I am worried about you. Please respond asap.

Simultaneously, Jerry emerged from his slumber and came to the door of the car, also wondering if I were safe.

By this time, I was trembling and near tears. I had distinctly felt danger, and my son and Jerry had also sensed this danger. *What the hell was going on?* I struggled to make sense of it all as I exited the car and went back into the motel room with Jerry. Once there, I curled up in his arms and fell asleep for a few hours. The next morning, we carried on as if the whole incident had never happened, and I am still unable to explain the events of that night.

Jerry and I continued to hang out together whenever I could get to Malibu, but our relationship eventually became strained. I grew weary of his lack of resources, and he became more and more irritable with me. I noticed he had started to show lesions on his skin that became worse and more prevalent over time. It appeared to me that he might be "skin popping," and I wanted nothing to do with hard drugs. Eventually, we went our separate ways, but I felt a tremendous sense of loss, as he was my first friend in Los Angeles.

Chapter 21

Khloe

In getting some distance from Jerry, I remembered that my real mission in coming to California this time was to save Khloe and Kendrick. I realized I needed to get going on this task, so I planned another trip to Los Angeles.

The day I planned to visit Khloe, I woke up with a renewed sense of purpose. I showered and dressed to the nines, appropriate for a Kardashian visit. I wore my best to meet her; blonde hair flowing in the sunshine and makeup done to perfection, including false eyelashes, a staple of celebrities. I wore an unstructured gray pinstripe suit with a white lace cami underneath, topped off by four-inch black heels, Birkin bag in tow, Submariner on my wrist, and diamonds in my ears and around my neck. I worked hard to give the impression that I belonged there.

Making my way from the Four Seasons Hotel to Khloe's gate was simple because of my car. I had no idea where the Kardashians lived, but fortunately, I had the magic car. After getting behind the wheel, I pulled up the navigation feature. The G-Wag spontaneously asked if I wanted it to take over the navigation, to which I said, "Yes."

The car set forth an itinerary and address for me to follow. I then allowed the car to take me by GPS on the 101 to the Kardashian gate.

The trip on the 101 wasn't difficult, but finding the gate was fascinating, given how hidden it was. There was no problem with the magic car. It was a seamless trip to visit her; I just needed an appointment, but I didn't let that stop me. Steve had told me that Khloe needed me, so I proceeded with as much confidence as I could summon.

I approached the palatial residential gate with mild intimidation. A steady stream of luxury cars, limos, and work vans raced in and out of the protected neighborhood of celebrities. I fit right in in my white G-Wag, just like Kris Jenner's at the time, so I blended in beautifully. I inched forward toward the guard.

"Hi. I'm here to see Khloe." I gave him my name and business card.

"Is she expecting you?" the guard asked.

"I believe so," I said confidently, for I truly believed I was sent there to save a suicidal Khloe.

I waited patiently while the guard called Khloe. He returned after a few moments. "Khloe says you are not scheduled on her calendar."

"Okay, no problem. I will touch base with her later," I said and proceeded through the massive gates, only to turn around and exit the compound.

After my rejection at the gate, I retreated from the Kardashian compound and returned to my hotel empty-handed. I just knew Khloe needed me, so I pulled over on the way back to say an earnest prayer for her well-being. I left her compound feeling comforted and like I had still accomplished something important.

Nothing in my day seemed out of the ordinary, as I took my job as a psychic healer to the stars very seriously. Fortunately, my communication from Steve in my hotel room continued, and it provided much comfort and guidance, and more assignments. Kendrick was next.

Chapter 22

Kendrick

After the rejection at the Kardashian gate, I traveled back to Seattle and tried to resume any semblance of a normal life. After a few weeks back home, I decided to fly back to California to embark on my continued healing journey as set forth from my Steve Jobs-guided televisions. My next mission after Khloe was to save Kendrick Lamar, whom my television indicated was at the end of his rope.

Los Angeles was the land of opportunity and promise. I was seeking a fresh start and trying to move away from pain and toward promise. Steve had told me by television vignettes that Kendrick was in trouble, burned out, and feeling low. I had been listening to his music obsessively and could literally feel his pain coming through his lyrics and haunting music, as it resonated with me. A boy from Compton had made it big, maybe too big, to sustain the lifestyle and empty façade of Hollywood, I surmised.

Previously, whenever I drove on the 101, I always said a prayer when I would pass Kendrick's exit. I could literally feel his energy, and believed he was reaching an impossible level of stress and misery, or so I perceived. I was excited to help him in any way I could.

Once back in Los Angeles and one morning at the hotel, I knew it was the time and place to find and help Kendrick. I dressed appropriately for the journey I was about to embark on, knowing I had to look good for him, yet not too flashy, as that was part of what Kendrick wanted to divest himself of.

After showering, I put on a pair of white jeans, white leather tennis shoes, a white silk cami, and a vintage Levi's jacket. Add to that some diamonds, a white Mercedes baseball cap worn backward, a Submariner, and an LV purse, and I was ready to go. I loved the look. Added to the cloudless day, I was happy and ready to roll to help Kendrick. I packed up a few things and headed to the magic car.

Chapter 23

Heavenly Cove

Once in the G-Wag, I turned on the navigation feature. A window immediately popped up, just like with Khloe, and asked if I wanted to let the car navigate for me. I said yes and headed to the 101 from the Four Seasons. I had planned to head south on the 101 toward Kendrick's exit, only this time I was directed to head north toward Malibu per my instructions from the car.

Having only visited California a few times, I had no idea where my car was taking me. I drove in light traffic to my destination. The scenery was just stunning, almost prehistoric. I exited the freeway and made my way down the mountainside to the northern part of Malibu.

The scenery on Kanan Road was stunning and terrifying as I approached Malibu. The road was lined with majestic peaks adjacent to terrifying cliffs down deep ravines. With one wrong move, I could easily slip off to my grave. I felt safe in the magic car, but still drove slowly as the locals whipped by me. The bottom of Kanan Road dead ends at PCH and Heavenly Cove, my destination per the GPS.

As I approached Heavenly Cove, a well-known, low-key resort compound in the heart of Malibu, I was blocked at the entrance by police cars, fire trucks, and ambulances. It looked like a parking lot just for emergency responders, and I could hardly enter the property. But the car's GPS directed me to follow the emergency vehicles and enter the compound.

I descended the driveway to the resort at sea level and gasped at the view before me. No fewer than ten fire trucks, fifteen ambulances, and innumerable police cars filled the parking lot and every available space, including the aisles and driveways.

A security gate was directly in front of me with a young man assisting with entry or denial. I inched toward him in relative shock that I had been led there by my car and had made it that far. I rolled down the window, and he asked, "How can I help you?"

Without forethought, I replied, "I've been asked to help with the situation."

The attendant released the gate and gestured for me to enter the mayhem. I inched into the compound and asked myself under my breath, *What the hell are you doing here, Liz?*

I couldn't go far into the parking lot due to the crowds of emergency vehicles, so I parked quickly and jumped out of my car. I walked slowly and surveyed the scene; something major was certainly going on. Customers from the resort stood outside the building in huddles, watching for any sign of celebrity, as is de rigueur in Los Angeles.

I approached a large group of emergency personnel in a huddle and walked directly and confidently to the one who looked like a leader. He looked directly at me and said, "How can I help you?"

Poised and without trepidation, I said, "I'm Liz. I'm here to help."

The captain looked deeply into my eyes, leaned toward me, and whispered, "Lady, we don't even know why we are here yet."

"I believe I know why you and I are here. There is a suicidal celebrity on this property, and we need to save him."

He looked more intently at me and smiled. "Hang on and stay here," he said as he turned back to his colleagues.

I stood there confidently as the captain consulted his comrades. He quickly came back to me and said, "Please be patient with us. We will know more soon."

I said, "Please take me to him when you can, sir," fully convinced Kendrick was there,

I stayed in place while the group disbursed. More and more emergency vehicles crowded the large parking lot, now making it impossible for me to leave, so I waited patiently for the captain to return. Just a few moments later, a service truck pulled up next to me with a handsome, middle-aged park ranger in it.

"Hi. I'm Matt. I'll take you where you need to go," he said.

I introduced myself and hopped in the truck. We drove through another guarded gate and entered a private neighborhood. The road was steep and windy, and occasionally, I could see the Pacific as we drove through a mature but modest neighborhood. We made our way up to the highest peak on the property and then drove due west to the road along the ocean.

Once hugging the cliffs over the sea, the park ranger slowed to a crawl. He said, "Just let me know where to stop," as we drove past low-key, oceanfront homes.

Me, tell you, where to stop? I thought. *That's a joke. I have no freaking idea.* I certainly couldn't let him know that detail.

So, I confidently said, "Stop just up here," as I motioned to a point in front of us on the edge of a cliff overlooking the ocean. I heard the ranger turn off the engine as I approached the edge of the cliff.

What the hell do I do now? I thought. I glanced back at the car and saw the ranger staring directly at me.

I looked north and south, up and down the craggy cliffs and to the roaring ocean below. I couldn't see another human. The only sound was the din of the crashing waves and a lone dog barking in the distance. I knew I had to act like I knew what I was doing, so I inched toward the cliff's edge and stretched out my arms up to the blue sky. I tilted my head to the sun, shut my eyes, and began to pray as if my life, and Kendrick's too, depended on it.

After about ten minutes of prayer, I withdrew my arms from the sun and turned on my heel back to the ranger's truck. I got into the passenger seat of the truck and smiled at Matt. "Thank you for bringing me up here," I said.

"Did you accomplish what you came up here for?" he asked.

"I did. Thank you," I replied as we started the long, windy journey back to the resort.

We drove in silence while I pondered what had just happened. *Had I made any difference? Was Kendrick here? Why did my car bring me to an emergency at Heavenly Cove?*

We approached the resort very slowly. As we descended into the main parking lot, I noticed that most of the emergency vehicles had left. Only a few cop cars and one fire truck were left.

Matt pulled up to the cop cars and said, "Here you go, Liz."

Did he really have to stop here? I thought. *What if the cops want to talk to me? Will I get in trouble? Will they arrest me?*

I exited the truck and came face-to-face with the captain I had spoken to earlier.

"Hey, Liz," he said to me. "Can we chat for a minute?" He motioned to an area away from the crowd.

"Sure," I said as my heart sank. *The jig is up. I'm going to be arrested*, I thought.

"Liz, my crew and I want to thank you for coming here today," the captain said.

What? You want to thank me? Holy crap!

"Whatever you did today really helped this situation. We can't thank you enough."

"Truly my pleasure," I said as I stuck out my hand to shake his.

He eagerly grabbed my hand with both hands and shook it vigorously. "I hope our paths cross again under different circumstances."

"Me, too," I replied as I turned away and walked toward my car that had been parked illegally for several hours.

Once inside, I repeated a long prayer for Kendrick and said a prayer of thanks to God for surviving the whole situation.

I drove slowly back to the Four Seasons in a daze. I was shocked at what I had just participated in and began to wonder if Steve Jobs really knew what he was talking about. *Was I really brought to California to save celebrities? Had I made any difference in my visits to help Kendrick and Khloe?* All I had were questions and no answers. I was suddenly overcome by insecurity and confusion. I decided to cut this trip to Los Angeles short and return to Seattle to consider my options.

Chapter 24

Back to Business

I returned to Seattle for a few weeks to contemplate my next move. I was feeling insecure about my role as psychic healer to celebrities, and the communication from Steve had waned. I decided it was time to shift my focus and visits to California to my latest business venture. I booked another flight to Los Angeles and resisted the urge to find Jerry, although I missed him every day. I chilled alone at the Four Seasons spa and pool for a couple of days, working on my new health and wellness company, which was in the early stages of development.

One morning, I woke up with a renewed sense of purpose and energy. I had a meeting scheduled that day at 1:00 p.m. with a man also staying at the hotel. One of the Four Seasons' bellhops had ascertained we were both in the same kind of business and thought we should meet. I dressed casually for lunch in the garden restaurant. A pale pink sundress, white strappy sandals, white jeans jacket, and a small, white Dior purse completed the look. The only jewelry I wore was a Submariner Rolex with a sapphire face.

I breezed into the restaurant, and the hostess guided me to a table with a good-looking, middle-aged man in a suit and tie, who rose to greet me with an outstretched hand. I extended my hand, and he vigorously shook it as the hostess pulled out my chair.

"Hello. I'm Bruce, so great to meet you. I see we have the same watch. This is a good sign."

I returned the greeting as we sat down, amused he immediately noticed our matching jewelry. Our table was next to a beautiful outdoor fountain, muffling our conversation from those seated around us. The waiter came quickly and filled our water glasses, and as he did, my lunchmate looked at me and said, "May I order for us?"

I tried to hide my surprise at his question and reflexively said, "Of course," instantly curious as to what he would choose.

"Robert, we would like two Grey Goose martinis and two blackened salmon Caesar salads," Bruce said to the waiter before he could give us menus.

I found it amusing that he ordered exactly what I would like, if it were dinner, and found myself warming to him instantly. Our conversation flowed effortlessly, and we found incredible synergies between our two companies and our respective goals. We finished our lunch by making a second date to get together.

Over the next three months on my visits to Los Angeles, Bruce and I continued our meetings, and he brought me into his fold of international colleagues in our area of business. We had similar business values and synergistic relationships, making it seem like a good idea to continue to associate with him. Despite my fragile emotional state, I believed I could vet this new relationship and hired him officially as a consultant.

As our mutual circle widened, Bruce helped me secure a manufacturer for my latest invention in healthcare and led me to a lab in San Diego to make my products. Little did I know what this team would later try to extract from me in exchange for his help. I thought the exorbitant fee I was paying him was the limits of our association.

Chapter 25

Business Building

Although I absolutely loved the Four Seasons chain, my bills there were racking up very quickly. To cut my expenses for future trips to California, I rented an Airbnb in West Los Angeles. I loaded the G-Wag with my suitcases and drove the short, but still somehow long trip into the city. I was pleased to see that the apartment was secure with locked gates and private, off-street parking, in addition to beautiful pools and a lush, tropical landscape. Inside, it was perfectly suitable with two bedrooms and two baths. The unit also had a beautiful interior balcony overlooking one of the pools. I was very pleased with myself as I could now pay for a month of rent for less than one week in a luxury hotel. Things seemed to be going my way at that point, and I was excited for my future.

Once settled in my new apartment, I lit a cigarette and contemplated my next move. I opened my laptop and logged on to the Wi-Fi. Immediately, Steve Jobs began his monologue movie, curated just for me. The images and sounds resonated with me as they showed me my future business success and dominance in my chosen career. It buoyed me and gave me incredible confidence for my future. As I sat there taking in all the information I was being presented, one of my cell phones rang with a number I didn't recognize. It startled me, but I quickly regained my composure and spoke, "Hello. Liz speaking."

"Hi, Liz. This is Ken from ABC Labs. I got your number from Bruce, who said you are looking for a laboratory to produce your health products. I have a specialty lab in San Diego and would like to invite you to come for a visit to our lab to meet with our chief chemist, Dr. Jose Ramirez."

"Hi, Ken. Nice to meet you. Thanks for the call," I replied.

"How about tomorrow at eleven?" Ken asked.

"That works for me," I replied.

"Perfect! I'll text our address to you. See you then," Ken finished.

I hung up the phone, and a smile spread across my face as I marveled at how well things seemed to be going for me at that moment.

I lit another cigarette as I headed to my car to buy some food at Trader Joe's. Once there, I loaded up on vegan provisions and hurried home to cook some food, as I was very hungry. I cooked a big pot of vegetable soup and ate a small bowl before falling asleep on the apartment's very comfortable couch.

Chapter 26
San Diego Lab

I woke up at 8:00 a.m. with a start after the deepest sleep I'd had in months. I couldn't believe I had been asleep for thirteen hours! I realized I had to be in San Diego soon, so I quickly ate a grapefruit and hopped in the shower. What should I wear for this very important meeting? I decided on casual elegance and picked an unstructured cream pantsuit with a pale-pink cami. Pearls, the Submariner, and flat sandals completed the look.

I hopped in the G-Wag and headed to the 405 to catch I-5 for the two-hour drive to San Diego. Traffic was unusually light, and I made the trip easily in under two hours. As I entered the business park, I saw an open space next to a black G-Wagon. As I rang the bell to enter the business, a gorgeous man opened the door and said, "Hi! You must be Liz. I'm Ken. Nice car, just like mine. Great minds must think alike!"

"Nice to meet you, Ken," I said as he vigorously shook my hand while leading me indoors.

The lab was smaller than I had expected and much more modest than previous labs I had worked with earlier in my career. Regardless, as Bruce - the consultant in whom I had placed my trust - had recommended the lab to me, I threw any concerns aside and took my seat in their small conference room.

"Liz, I'd like you to meet Dr. Ramirez, our chief chemist and formulator," Ken said as Dr. Ramirez walked into the conference room. "I see you both have the same watch! This must be a good sign."

I was amused at the second watch reference and stood to shake his hand. He took his seat directly across from me at the table. "Please call me Jose," he said as he sat down.

Jose was a short, stout man with a very pleasant demeanor. Ken indicated there would be another physician from Los Angeles joining us for the meeting, a world expert in the type of business I was building. I was confused by the surprise addition to our meeting and wondered who would show up.

It didn't take long for Dr. Dreamy to appear: tall, very fit, shaggy-blonde hair, tanned skin, and bright-blue eyes. He was certainly the most attractive physician I had ever laid eyes on, that was for sure. Dr. Dreamy didn't say much during the meeting, but kept his beautiful eyes trained on me for the entire time we were together. Although it was highly distracting, I managed to conduct a productive meeting and accomplish my goals.

After donning protective clothing and shoe covers, Dr. Ramirez gave me a one-on-one tour of the lab where we finalized the ingredients in my first five products. Afterward, I met up with Dr. Dreamy and

Ken in the conference room. I thanked the gentlemen for their time and asked for an ETA of my products.

"We should have these completed for you by next week," Ken said as he shook my hand.

I was very pleased with the turnaround time and told him so.

I turned to Dr. Dreamy and extended my hand to say goodbye. Instead of shaking my hand, he grabbed it and led me out of the room and toward the door. Once outside, and still holding my hand, he said, "Hey, Liz, you are incredibly smart and are obviously going to lead this field. I think we should pair up. How about dinner tomorrow night in Los Angeles?" he asked.

Thinking of nothing but rainbows and unicorns at being asked out by Dr. Dreamy, I reflectively said, "That would be great!"

"Perfect. Meet me at Nobu Malibu at seven," he finished as he opened the door for me to the G-Wag.

"I see you got the right car for the job," he finished as he waved goodbye to me as I backed out of the parking space.

"Apparently so, and the right watch, too," I shouted out the window as I drove off.

I found it amusing and a little odd that my colleagues noticed these tangible similarities of our possessions and wondered if it were a good sign. The trip back to Los Angeles was grueling: hot, slow, and long. Traffic was a nightmare, but I didn't mind as I was buoyed by the productive trip and my upcoming dinner date.

Chapter 27
Dinner with Dr. Dreamy

I woke up on D-Day with a new excitement. I couldn't believe I had found a lab to make my products, a consultant to help me navigate the Los Angeles business waters, and a date with Dr. Dreamy at my favorite restaurant. A trifecta of blessings I so desperately needed at that point in my life.

I showered and put on one of my favorite outfits: a black jumpsuit with a halter top that showed off my collarbones and newly slim arms. I paired the outfit with black platform sandals and a multicolored cashmere pashmina, just in case it got cold in the evening. I hopped in the G-Wag and drove the hour's drive to Nobu Malibu.

After parking, I entered the bar to wait for my date. I scanned the small area and looked for a place to sit. There was no room, so I exited the bar to the outdoor seating area and literally ran into Dr. Dreamy, who was coming in the same door I was exiting.

"Hey, Liz!" Dr. Dreamy said as he gave me a warm embrace. "You made it!"

"Of course I did!" I replied.

"I've got a table for us outside," he said as he led me to the best outdoor table at the restaurant, the same one I had enjoyed with Sergi.

"This is beautiful. I absolutely love this place," I said as I viewed the Pacific Ocean next to our table.

"Not nearly as beautiful as you are, Liz," he said in reply.

Did he just say that? He is the most handsome doctor I have ever seen! What on earth does he see in me?

I was instantly uncomfortable with the attention and stare of his blue eyes, but I didn't let on. The evening flew by, and Dr. Dreamy asked me lots of questions about my formulas and my knowledge of our mutual industry. At times, I wondered if he was trying to steal my expertise, but quickly quelled those fears as I had been told he was a world expert. *What could he possibly want from me professionally?* I thought.

Our meal was fabulous, and the sunset was perfect. After dinner, he ordered us aperitifs and paid the bill. As we walked to our cars, he asked if he could see me again. I thought it was incredibly sweet and chivalrous of him to invite me on another date, and I quickly said yes. He gave me a long hug and a big kiss on the lips as we parted. He was an incredible kisser, and my knees were weak as we pulled away from our embrace.

As I hopped in the G-Wagon, I noticed Dr. Dreamy getting into an old, dented Toyota truck, out of keeping with the usual cars at Nobu. I wondered how successful he really could be driving such an old car in Los Angeles, but then quickly shamed myself for the thought. I was excited to see Dr. Dreamy again, and our next planned date was set for the day I was going to pick up my product samples in San Diego.

Chapter 28

Snakes in the Lab

I busied myself in Los Angeles over the next week and spent quite a bit of time working on my business back in Seattle. Additionally, buoyed by the partnership with the lab in San Diego, I worked on my new business.

I spent hours on end creating massive PowerPoint presentations to present to future investors in my new company.

I met with and hired a powerful CPA, formerly with L'Oréal, who analyzed my company's financials and business plan and gave my start-up company a $200 million, pre-money valuation. This was an incredibly positive turn in my life, and I couldn't wait to pick up my first five products at the lab. On this visit to California, I was feeling stable, hopeful, and optimistic about my life.

On the day I was to pick up my products in San Diego, I couldn't wait to get to the lab. I dressed casually in all white for the meeting and prepared for the drive. This time, traffic was fierce as I headed south, and I barely made it on time. As I pulled into the parking lot, I noticed

Ken's black G-Wag and Dr. Dreamy's truck. I didn't know that Dreamy would be at the meeting, but I was excited to see him twice in one day.

After the requisite handshakes, we took our seats in the conference room. This time, Dr. Dreamy sat directly across from me and didn't break his stare for the entire meeting. Ken, the owner of the lab, led the meeting with Dr. Ramirez. I waited anxiously as they brought out my products one by one and showed me their exceptional work on my formulas. Every single formula was better than the next, and I was genuinely impressed with their work and told them so.

After a full product review and discussion of the prices and timing for larger product runs, the conversation went silent. I looked at Ken, Dr. Ramirez, and finally Dr. Dreamy. No one spoke, but all three looked directly at me. I suddenly felt a cold draft in the room and got a pit in my stomach. *What is going on here? Why is no one talking? Am I supposed to say something?*

At that point, after a long, silent pause, Dr. Dreamy took the floor. "Liz, we have really enjoyed working with you." It seemed like an unnecessary sweeping statement given that we had only known each other for a week, introduced by Bruce, the consultant I had hired at the Four Seasons. "We would like to continue to work with you."

"That's great because I would really like to work with you all, too," I replied, a sentiment I thought was obvious given I had hired them to produce my products. At this point, it dawned on me that I had not ever received back a signed copy of my mutual non-disclosure agreement, putting my intellectual property at risk.

Dr. Dreamy continued, "We think you are creating the definitive company in this untapped market, and we would like to be your partner."

I glanced around the table and realized all eyes were on me at that point. I began to get sick to my stomach, and I felt my skin begin to warm. *What does he mean by partner?*

"Of course, we will be partners; you will be my manufacturer," I replied.

"By partner, we mean equity partners in *your* company. We are willing to work with you in exchange for 51 percent equity in your company," he finished.

Fifty-one percent of my company that was just valued at $200 million dollars? I thought to myself and began to panic.

I looked first at Dr. Ramirez, but he averted his gaze as soon as our eyes met. I then turned my attention to Ken. "I don't understand, Ken. We have never discussed an equity partnership in my company. I hired your lab and paid you to create formulas using my expertise and knowledge. What is going on here?"

He deflected my question and deferred to Dr. Dreamy. Dr. Dreamy's sheen was wearing off, and I suddenly saw him as a pariah hoping to steal my efforts and intellectual property. His gorgeous smile and handsome countenance had turned into a frown that needed Botox. I searched his face for the warm, flirty demeanor I had enjoyed at Nobu, but it was gone.

"Liz, we want to work with you, but we need that equity in your company to do so," he stated without expression.

I had not predicted this turn of events and suddenly felt scared, vulnerable, and overwhelmed. These three men, whom I thought were my business friends, had become my adversaries. My new partners had become my competitors. I couldn't believe what was happening at that moment.

As I had paid up-front for the sample run of my first five products, I let the group know that my company wasn't up for grabs, and I was not offering equity under any circumstances. I stood up from the table and asked Ken to load the products into my car.

As I left the room, Dr. Dreamy followed me out to the car. "Hey, Liz, we *really* want to work with you," he said as he opened my door.

"Well, Dr. Dreamy, then simply make my products for me," I replied.

He ignored my statement. "Let us know when you change your mind," he said as he closed my door and leaned in the open window. "I look forward to seeing you tonight for dinner. Six o'clock at Spago."

I couldn't believe he truly expected me to join him for dinner after what we just went through. I had no intention of seeing him - ever again - and found some just satisfaction in standing him up that evening. The drive back to Los Angeles was brutal, made more so by the tears streaming down my face all the way. I was in shock from what I had experienced, and now my business was set back by months.

I called my consultant, Bruce, as soon as I got back to the apartment. He didn't pick up the phone, so I left him a terse message, which he never answered. More money, time, and trust had been wasted in a business where the first-mover advantage was rapidly slipping away. I felt like I had hit rock bottom in business. I felt hopeless again and cried myself to sleep.

Chapter 29
The Salesman

After the incident at the San Diego lab, I went to bed, put the covers over my head, and cried for what seemed like hours. I felt—and was—all alone in a strange city, trying to start a new company while swimming upstream in shark-infested waters. I intuitively knew I was out of my league, but I refused to accept defeat.

After a few days of languishing in bed, I finally opened my computer. There, I found a message on LinkedIn from a salesman in my industry. He offered to help me with my skincare project and indicated his fee would come from the contacts and introductions he would make for me. At that time, his offer sounded incredibly attractive as I was feeling financially insecure and had just experienced a significant setback with the crew in San Diego.

The salesman's proposal sounded very good to me at that moment, and he and I quickly exchanged electronic signatures on my blanket non-disclosure agreement. I sent him a copy of my latest PowerPoint presentation and let him know of the pre-money valuation I had received from the CPA. Soon thereafter, we planned a trip to Colorado to meet with a "big fish" in my area of business.

Chapter 30
Colorado

The salesman and I met at the Denver airport and took an Uber together to our meeting. The lab was in Boulder and was an impressive display of modern technology and financial might. The facility looked both inspiring and intimidating to me. I hadn't known what the dress code would be in Colorado, so I played it safe with a black pantsuit, pink lace cami, pearls, Submariner, and two-inch black heels.

After providing our identification to the secretary, we were asked to sign an electronic, mutual nondisclosure agreement before leaving the reception area. A few moments later, an ebullient, powerful-looking man in an Armani suit greeted us.

"Hello. You must be Liz," he said to me as he outstretched his hand, revealing his own Submariner on his right wrist. "Nice watch!"

"Hi, John. So lovely to meet you," I replied.

John turned to the salesman and said, "Hey, so great to see you again! Come on back."

The salesman and I spent several hours with John as he took us on a tour of his incredible facility. Although I had worked with many labs previously, this was by far the most impressive facility and setup I had ever seen in the U.S. John spent his time romancing us, attempting to win over my business.

"You won't find a better lab than us for your business," John stated repeatedly during our visit.

The time with John at his lab flew by, and soon he indicated he needed to attend another meeting. I was crestfallen when he didn't have time to see my brand presentation, but buoyed when John invited us to visit him and his "real lab" in his hometown of Houston, Texas.

"Hey, y'all, I've got to go now, but I would like to meet with you again in Houston, where I have my *big* lab," John stated. "We have over five hundred thousand square feet there, and I think you will be impressed with our capabilities and capacities. I'd really like to work with you, Liz."

I had a hard time thinking another lab could be more impressive than this one in Boulder, but the salesman indicated that John was right. Houston was where it was at. Before we left the lab for the day, we three made a future date to meet in Texas, about four weeks hence.

Chapter 31
One Night in Boulder

The salesman and I decided to celebrate our good fortune in meeting with John with a night out on the town. We took an Uber from John's lab to the Airbnb where the salesman had rented us a home for our one night in Boulder. Once there, we took a quick tour around the house and scoped out our respective bedrooms.

The house in Boulder was sweet and charming, with new age crystals of various shapes and sizes scattered throughout the home, resting on every available surface. I played with a few crystals in my hand while waiting for the salesman to change his clothes. I felt a significant energy in the home and surmised it was benevolent, given the crystals.

The salesman and I took another Uber to the downtown area of Boulder and had an incredible dinner at Steakhouse No. 316, made more divine with a bottle of Cristal champagne and Cakebread Napa Cabernet. After dinner, we walked to a few more restaurants, where we continued our celebratory drinking, enjoying bottle after bottle of amazing wine. Finally, around midnight, we made our way home via another Uber.

The salesman and I quickly retired to our respective rooms for the night. I fell asleep with ease but woke up wide awake a few hours later. I tossed and turned for a while before deciding to give up the fight for sleep and decided to wander. I left my bedroom and headed toward the sliding glass door leading to the backyard. As I approached the glass, I noticed a very odd yellow light outside. It looked like a strange dawn, but the clock told me it was only three o'clock in the morning.

Before going outside, I decided to collect as many crystals as possible from the home to take with me. I gathered crystal after crystal of all types and stuffed them into my pockets and arms. As I did so, I felt an immediate surge of energy flow through my body, almost as if I had consumed a pot of coffee. I was fully awake at this point.

I opened the door to the backyard and stood on the patio for what seemed like a long time. I gazed to the right and noticed a large wooden shed, so I elected to investigate further. As I approached the shed, a skull of a cow with intact horns appeared before me on the side of the building. As I drew closer to the head, it began to talk to me in the voice and style of Georgia O'Keeffe, one of my artistic heroes. Georgia was laughing and calling out to me to "join the celebration."

As I reached out to touch the cow skull, a flock of small birds, which I hadn't previously appreciated, suddenly took flight from the bush adjacent to the shed. The birds, two of whom were Anthony Bourdain and Kate Spade, began to talk and sing to me, beckoning me to join them in song and celebration. Seeing no reason to rebuff their offer, I too began to dance and sing with my departed friends.

Anthony and Kate let me know they were happy and loving life on the other side. They indicated death is not to be feared but celebrated. As I continued to revel with my heroes, I was suddenly awakened back to reality by the touch of the salesman's hand on my shoulder.

"Liz, what the hell are you doing out here at this hour?" he asked in a whispered voice of concern.

"I'm hanging out with my friends," I replied as I gestured to the shed and bush.

"Liz, you are the only one out here at four o'clock in the morning," he replied. "You need to come in now. We will have to leave for the airport soon."

I was crestfallen at the interruption. I protested a little, but fortunately realized I really wanted to preserve this relationship with the salesman, so I'd better get back inside with him.

We walked arm in arm back into the house. I placed the crystals back into their respective homes and went back to bed. The next day, we carried on as though nothing out of the ordinary had happened that night. We parted ways at Denver International after making plans to meet again in Houston.

Chapter 32

Houston, We Have a Problem

The salesman and I met a month later in Houston. We rented a car and drove the long drive to John's "big lab." The security at this facility was even tighter, and it took us quite a bit of time to get cleared for our visit. I had decided to pull out the stops for this meeting and had borrowed a gorgeous black Chanel dress and red stiletto Louboutins from a dear friend back home.

Our meeting was scheduled for one o'clock in the afternoon, and we arrived in plenty of time. We waited alone in the fancy lobby, assuming John would be on time, like he was previously in Colorado. We continued to wait as other guests filed in and were taken back behind the locked door before us. I expressed my concern to the salesman as we had to get back to George Bush Airport for our respective departing flights.

"Don't worry, Liz," the salesman said. "This meeting is worth the wait, even if we have to change our flights home."

In preparation for this meeting, I had worked diligently on my best PowerPoint presentation, including the information about my company's pre-money valuation. I had also spent quite a bit of time researching John online and had surmised he was the perfect partner for my now international business plan. He was rich, powerful, and already a global leader in the type of business I had started. I anxiously awaited our meeting.

Finally, at nearly three o'clock, John burst through the door into the lobby and ushered us back. "Hey y'all, I'm so sorry for the wait. I had an emergency meeting with my partners from Mexico," he stated. "Have a seat." He pointed to fancy chairs around a beautiful mahogany table. I sat down and opened my laptop to show John my presentation.

"John, shall I project my presentation for you?" I asked, looking at his sophisticated tech setup in the conference room.

"No, I don't have time for that today," he replied.

Don't have time for my presentation today? I flew the two of us here ... for what? You kept me waiting for hours for this? Why am I wearing this incredible dress and insane shoes? I thought.

I didn't have to say anything before John sat down next to me and said, "Let's see what you got."

I started to review my presentation, which was about thirty pages long, but John grew immediately impatient. "Can I take control of the presentation?" he asked as he reached to touch my Mac.

"Of course, John, I know your time is scarce," I replied, grateful he was at least looking at my hard work.

John scrolled through the pages of my presentation like a driver on a racetrack, glossing over the weeks and months of agonizing work I had put into my business plan. Occasionally, he would pause and say, "This looks good," or "This looks great!" Other than that, he didn't ask any questions or say much else.

Confused, I looked at the salesman, who gave me a thumbs-up sign. I waited patiently as John sped through my entire brand presentation in about five minutes.

After he finished, John stood up from the table and offered us water. He left the conference room and returned with three bottles of still Perrier, which we all started to drink in unison. I could feel the air change as we sat there, and John's boisterous personality turned somber. I looked at the salesman for guidance, but none was forthcoming from him. He looked as confused as I was at this point in the meeting.

John sat across from me at the vast table. He looked intently at me with his incredible blue eyes and didn't say anything for a long time. Finally, he spoke. "Liz, you have put together the most impressive, comprehensive business plan I have ever seen in our respective industry. I have a proposal for you."

I wasn't sure what kind of proposal he had in his mind, but I was certainly going to listen to him, given the expense and effort I had spent getting in front of him.

"I would like to be more than your partner here," he said while maintaining his gaze at me.

"I'm listening," I replied, trying to maintain a poker face.

"I would like to offer you one billion dollars for your entire company and business plan. I would then like you to stay on as chief executive officer for as long as you would like, but a minimum of two years," he offered. "You will need to move to Houston or Boulder as well."

I couldn't believe what I was hearing. *A billion dollars is incredible! But do I want to lose control of my company? Do I want to move to Colorado or Texas?* All I had were questions at that point, but John was very short on time and let me know so again.

"John, I didn't come here to sell my company," I replied as quickly as I could form the answer in my mind.

"We would love to be your partner, regardless," he stated. "This offer won't come around again, so if you say no today, it's off the table."

"I am flattered at the offer, for sure," I replied, "but I am not interested in selling today."

"Sounds great. I look forward to working with you," John finished as he led us out of the conference room back to the lobby. On my way out of the building, I noticed a massive wall hanging of a photo of John standing beside his Gulfstream g550 and wondered if I had made the right decision.

On the drive back to the Houston airport, the salesman told me I had indeed made the right decision. He believed, as I did, that my company was ultimately worth *well over* one billion dollars. After leaving Houston, I flew back to Los Angeles, and I worked as hard as I could in the ensuing months to bring forth the fruits of my efforts and launch a successful business on my own, as laid out in my business plan.

Despite my labile moods and erratic sleep schedule, I truly believed I was up for the task of creating, growing, and running a business potentially valued at a billion or more dollars.

Chapter 33
The Billionaire

I slowly came to and realized something was wrong, terribly wrong. With my eyes still closed to block the intense light above me, I began to awaken to my reality. I was lying on the floor of a jail cell.

I was freezing and in pain from the cement floor that had housed me for an undetermined amount of time. I got up from the floor and moved toward the locked door. A tiny window was looking out onto a cold, gray hallway, with not a human in sight. I turned around and noticed I must have been put in a holding cell, as there was no toilet. I was completely alone and had to pee.

I started to scream for help while staring out the window. No one initially answered my pleas. It seemed like an eternity before a stocky, gruff warden appeared outside the cell.

"What do you want?" she asked me, looking very annoyed that she had to attend to me.

"Where am I?" I asked her.

"You're in jail," she replied in an irritated tone.

No duh, I thought to myself. "How did I get here?" I asked.

"You're in Santa Monica. You were picked up by the police. They found you passed out in the middle of the street."

What the fuck? Passed out in the middle of the street in Los Angeles? I was shocked. But what was more disturbing was that I had no recollection of what had happened.

"Where is my purse?" I asked.

"You didn't have a purse when the cops picked you up," the warden replied.

"Great …" I mumbled. Gone was my new Mercedes purse and wallet, along with $2,000 cash, my new iPhone, my Platinum AmEx, and my driver's license. *How will I ever get that back?* I thought to myself.

"When can I get out of here?" I asked.

"We have contacted your son, and he is on the way to pick you up," she finished.

My son? How did they know how to reach him? They don't even know my name, let alone my son's name or number. Nothing was making sense, and my body hurt more and more by the minute as I gradually came out of my altered state. My clothes were wet and disheveled, and I had a massive headache.

The warden left and I returned to the floor. I felt like I was in the Twilight Zone, with no memory of what had happened to land me in jail. I scoured my mind for any clue to help me put this situation together.

The night before, I had gone alone to have a drink at Malibu City Grill in Malibu. I had recently traveled back to Los Angeles and had just finished a long day of work on my new business venture, and I wanted to get out and socialize for a little while. The restaurant was packed with people and the atmosphere was lively. I approached the bar and ordered a drink, Grey Goose on the rocks. I scanned the bar area for an empty seat and saw only one seat open at a table with a good-looking, jovial couple.

As I approached their table, I noticed the beautiful woman seemed much younger than the man, which is not an uncommon sight in Los Angeles. I also thought I recognized the man as a business titan and famous billionaire, often in the public eye, and recalled that we were "friends" on LinkedIn.

"May I put my drink down on your table for a moment?" I asked them.

They both smiled at me and said, "Yes."

The young woman went on to say, "Don't worry. We won't roofie you."

Now that's a weird thing to say, I thought to myself, but I brushed it off and took a sip of my drink, although grateful that they had clarified that point.

"Have a seat and join us," the man said.

So, I did. "What kind of work do you do?" I asked the man.

"I'm in logistics," he said.

Hmmm, logistics... I knew what that meant, and it confirmed that this man was who I thought he was. Because he was rich and famous, I trusted him and the situation I was in.

I looked around the packed bar and marveled at all the activity. Los Angeles, and Malibu in particular, was beginning to feel more familiar to me. I was excited at the prospect of making new friends, like this couple at the table.

For the next half hour, everything seemed copacetic as we made small talk. Then things got weird. I excused myself from the table and said I was going to the bathroom. Once there, the young woman followed me into the stall and started grabbing my breasts and rubbing my ass. She asked if I swung both ways, to which I said no. It was uncomfortable to say the least, but I tried not to offend her. The woman followed me back to the table, and we resumed polite conversation, acting as if nothing had happened.

"Hey, do you want to join us tonight at a Hollywood party?" the man asked me.

"Sure!" I said, never thinking the worst.

What could be wrong with this innocent party invite from a world-famous billionaire?

"Awesome! We are just about to leave. We can take one car," he said.

We finished our drinks and exited the restaurant. As we left, the waitstaff jockeyed for the opportunity to hold the door open for us and gave us a cheery goodbye.

"Thanks for coming in, Bob!" they nearly said in unison, completely ignoring his companion and me.

Chapter 34
The Hollywood Party

I had parked my car with the restaurant valet, and we agreed we would all come back after the party to get our cars. I had heard the valet say the man owned the neon Lamborghini in the parking lot, and I wondered how the three of us would fit in it.

"We are going to take her car," he said, referring to the young woman's beat-up BMW being pulled up by the valet staff.

"Okay, I need to get something in my car before I go," I said.

I ran over to the G-Wag in the vast parking lot and removed my passport from my new purse and placed it in the center console. I have no idea why I did this, but thankfully, I did.

When I purchased the G-wagon at Calabasas Mercedes, they generously gave me a beautiful Argentinian leather purse and wallet, which I had taken with me that night. I took my purse with me in the car to the Hollywood party. I was seated in the back seat of her coupe, and the two of them sat in the front seats.

As we pulled out of the restaurant parking lot heading south on the US1 toward Santa Monica, I started to not feel well. Her driving was erratic and sloppy, but the two of them seemed to like the danger aspect of it all. As we rounded the turn toward Santa Monica, I began to fade and lose consciousness. I have no recollection of arriving at the party.

The next semi-lucid moment I had was of walking through throngs of people at a raging party, complete with loud, pounding music and a disco ball with seizure-inducing strobe lights. The man had his arm around my waist and was leading me through the crowd, and the masses were all chanting his name in unison, "Bob, Bob, Bob!" It was a moment of coherence for me, just long enough to experience my head slamming to the ground and being shoved underwater. That is the last thing I remember.

Apparently, the couple disposed of my unconscious body at some point that evening on a street in Santa Monica, not Hollywood, where the party had taken place. They stole my new purse, wallet, driver's license, cash, credit cards, and phone. After I got out of jail, I messaged the man on LinkedIn, asking for my purse back. His response was to block me. Classy.

By the grace of God, this man died in a tragic accident not too long after this event in my life. It couldn't have happened to a "nicer" billionaire.

I spent the next several days trying to get my life back on track, replacing my AmEx and phone while being in a very fragile, confused state.

I tried for the next month to report the incident to the police. First, I went to the Malibu police. I thought because the crime had taken place in the Malibu restaurant, that would be the place to go. Once there, I was told I had to report it to the Santa Monica police because that was where the police picked me up.

In the Santa Monica precinct, I was told I had to report the crime in Malibu. I literally got nowhere with a police report and was later told by a local resident that this particular billionaire had bought off all the cops in Los Angeles and Malibu, where he lived. I have no idea if that were true, but I had no luck in filing a report once I mentioned his name.

This whole incident shook me to my core. I returned to Seattle for a few weeks before "restarting" my business meetings in Los Angeles, vowing to trust no one as I forged ahead all alone. Once home, Steve Jobs continued to guide me and encouraged me to continue my business pursuits in SoCal. I soon planned another trip.

Chapter 35

Lost

The truth is that I have no idea how I got to where I ended up that day, and years later, I still don't.

As usual, the California sun was shining brightly, highlighting the deep blue sky above Los Angeles that I loved so much. At first, I didn't even know what town I was in. All I knew was I was on a mission to save people, as Steve Jobs directed.

I walked for what seemed like miles in bare feet, thankful it wasn't raining or too hot, but it was still early morning. I was dressed and disheveled in white jeans and a white tank top. I didn't have my phone or my purse. I was truly anonymous and had no way to identify myself.

I stopped along my walk in this strange town and rested at a bus stop. My life seemed surreal. I felt hungry and couldn't remember the last time I had eaten or had any water. I put my hands in my jeans pocket and realized I had no money and no way to get money. I felt completely alone and confused. I struck up a conversation with a beautiful black man at the bus stop; he listened to my tale of woe and handed me a $5 bill as he stood up to get on the approaching bus. I couldn't thank him enough and simultaneously couldn't believe I had just taken money from a stranger, a first for me.

Once the bus departed, I walked further along the sidewalk to a strip mall where there was a convenience store. I knew the most important thing was water, so I spent the entire five dollars buying two small bottles of water. I had no money left for food, so I left the store and walked back to the bus stop. This time, there was a new man there, hunched over what looked like a stolen shopping cart. He was dressed in all black, with dark hair, light brown skin, a Fedora hat, and what looked to me like fake facial hair. I walked past him and instantly noted that his cart was empty, not typical for a homeless person who usually carries their worldly possessions with them at all times in such transportation.

"Hey, what's your name?" he asked me as I walked by him.

I kept walking a few more feet and then decided to stop and address him. I figured I had nothing to lose as I was pretty much homeless myself at that point and had never been afraid of homeless people.

"My name is Liz," I said. "What's yours?"

"Roger," he replied. "I haven't seen you around. What are you doing here?"

Good Lord, how do I answer that? I had no idea where I was or how I got there. I also had no idea where I was going or how to get there with no phone, no money, and no ID.

I decided to turn back toward Roger and take a good look at him. All I could think about in my paranoid state was he was a spy or a plant, put there to keep tabs on me. I looked intently at him and noticed more weird things. He was wearing a Rolex watch, designer clothes under the fancy, too-big overcoat, and high-end, polished shoes, not in keeping with a homeless man. His hair was longish, thick, and very dark. His black eyes were piercing in their gaze. He looked like a wealthy man trying to pretend he was not.

"I'm not sure why I'm here," I said. "Why are you here?"

"I am waiting for my father to get out of surgery," he said as he motioned to the building across the street. "That's a hospital."

Chapter 36

Roger

In my dazed state, I hadn't even noticed there was a hospital nearby. It gave me a sense of comfort knowing that I could always go there if I got desperate.

"Where are you from?" Roger asked me.

"I'm from Washington State," I answered. "What about you?"

"Brazil. My family and I traveled here for my dad's heart surgery. Would you like a cup of coffee?"

Are you kidding me? I thought to myself.

"I would love one," I replied.

"Great. Let's walk down to the corner store," he said.

Once back at the corner convenience store, we sat at an outside table. Roger went into the store and brought back two steaming cups of coffee. He had added the perfect amount of cream without asking me how I took my coffee. There was a weird familiarity with him, like

I had known him in another lifetime, or was it this lifetime? I truly had no idea what I was doing in this strange city.

Our conversation was lighthearted and casual. Roger asked me lots of questions about living in the United States, and I was struck by how good his English was, hardly an accent.

After about thirty minutes, Roger indicated he needed to head back to the hospital. I stayed at the table and watched him push the shopping cart away from where we were sitting and toward the hospital.

"Hey, Liz, will you be here later?" he asked.

"Definitely," I said.

"I'll see you later," he said as he drove the empty cart along the sidewalk.

"Nice meeting you, Roger. Thank you for the coffee!" I shouted.

As I sat in the shade on what would be a very hot day, I tried to figure out what had happened to bring me to this suburb of Los Angeles. It was unfamiliar to me and seemed far away from where I was staying. And, I had no recollection of going there, either previously or on that day.

With no shoes, phone, ID, or money, there was little I could do with myself in this strange city. I decided to head over to the hospital myself and see if I could get any help there.

As I walked to the hospital, I wondered if I would see Roger again. Given that I was barefoot, I decided against walking into the hospital. I tried to avoid the hot pavement, but it was nearly impossible, and I started to get blisters on the soles of my feet.

I decided to walk the entire perimeter of the hospital before deciding what to do next. After I had nearly completed the walk, I noticed an open door to the basement of the building.

Lacking the foresight to determine this was not a great idea, I entered through the door.

Chapter 37
The Hospital

As a former physician and one-time hospital employee, I had been in the basement of a hospital before, so it seemed oddly familiar, with boilers, furnace, wood shop, metal shop, laundry and linens, and so forth. I hid in a corner near the door and looked for any signs of life. It appeared that I was alone.

I scoured the area to see where I could go next and saw an exit sign and a sign for "stairs." I quickly sprinted to the door and helped the door shut quietly behind me. As I turned around in the stairwell, all I saw was an interminable metal staircase upward.

Thankfully, I was in really good shape, not intentionally, mind you. My body had seemed to flip a switch from my days of fighting with my weight. Recently, I had been able to eat anything I wanted while still losing weight, but it seemed my appetite had lessened significantly in sunny California. I had boundless energy, and my muscles were lean and obvious under my emaciated frame. It never occurred to me to worry about my new metabolism. For me, it was a "cause célèbre."

I listened carefully up the stairwell to make sure there were no people in the area. I leaped up the stairs quickly and felt proud of how fit I was. I managed to avoid any other humans and easily reached the roof of the building many floors up.

So here I was, on the rooftop of a hospital building in a California suburb, thinking this was a perfectly normal activity. I spent a couple of hours there, picking up various treasures such as nuts, bolts, wire, and cardboard. Somehow, I believed these were very important items that everyone else had failed to see. I stuffed what I could of my new treasures into my pockets and bra and decided to head southward. Only one critical step had been missed: what to do about the door that locked behind me when I stepped out on the roof.

As I got to the locked door, my heart sank. I realized what had happened and knew I was in trouble. *How in God's name could I explain why I was barefoot and on the roof? Would I be found out? Be arrested (again)? How would I reach someone? How long would I be stranded on the roof with no shade from the beating sun?* I began to panic. I decided to sit down away from the door.

It seemed like forever, but about an hour later, a maintenance worker exited the door to the roof. He walked right past me and headed to the other side of the roof. I bolted to my feet and grabbed the door just before it closed shut. I hurried into the stairwell and began my descent.

Halfway down the stairs, a group of nurses entered the stairwell. I turned around and ran back upstairs several floors and waited until they had exited the stairwell.

Whew! That was a close call, I thought to myself. I knew the only way out of the building for me was the way I came in, through the basement. The only problem was that there were workers in there now.

I poked my head into the basement from the stairwell and saw a group of four men chatting near the metal shop. I waited for about fifteen minutes before they disbursed, and I could leave the building. As I exited the building, I decided to divest myself of most of the treasures I had acquired on the roof. I believed they were important artifacts, so I carefully placed them in the bushes outside the hospital and promised myself I would return to fetch them later.

The sun was directly overhead, so I surmised it was about noon. If the sun hadn't told me, I would have figured it out based on my hunger. I had finished the water I had bought with the money from the man at the bus, and I now had no resources for food.

Chapter 38

Foraging for Food

On my way back to the convenience store, I had to pass the bus stop where I had met Roger. I scoured the area for him but didn't see him. I figured he was still with his father at the hospital. I arrived at the store and sat down at the same sidewalk table where Roger and I had coffee. I was becoming a regular there that day, and it gave me a little sense of belonging, if only for a moment.

I knew I couldn't go back inside the store, as I was barefoot. Somehow, I had escaped the "no shirt, no shoes, no service" policy on my first visit that day to buy water. But now there were too many people and eyeballs on me to go in. It didn't matter anyway, as I had no money to purchase anything. I knew I probably couldn't stay there indefinitely, so I kept my empty water bottle on the table in front of me as a decoy.

After about twenty minutes, a group of boisterous young men approached the store on skateboards. The roar of the kids on their boards en masse was deafening, and the boys were shouting excitedly at each other as they approached.

The boys—about eight of them—all seemed to be around fourteen years old. They pulled chairs from a few outdoor tables, and all sat together at the table next to me. I listened to their conversation about their world travel during a recent school break and realized these were privileged kids. Having raised two boys of my own, I knew how to relate to these guys. I struck up a conversation with the boy closest to me, hoping I could curry a favor and borrow some cash to get some food.

"Are you having fun today?" I asked.

"Yes, we got out of school early today!" the young man replied.

"Where do you go to school?" I asked.

"We go to Saint Joseph's," he replied.

Even being from out of town, I had heard of this nationally known, private prep school. *These are probably good kids*, I thought. They started playing pop music on one of their phones, and I joined them in singing the lyrics of some of my favorite songs.

"Hey! You are cool!" one of the boys said to me.

"Thank you," I said. "You guys are pretty cool yourselves."

I thought it was awesome, I knew their music, and it made me miss the days of listening to pop music with my own kids, now grown and on their own.

What appeared to be the ringleader of the pack stood up and declared to the group that he was going to go inside to get some food. On his way to the door, he came over to me, stuck out his hand to shake mine, and said, "Hi! I'm Lucas."

I was struck by both his good looks and his manners. "Hi, Lucas. I'm Liz," I replied.

He had a firm handshake and smiled brightly at me. "Can I bring you something to eat, Liz?"

OMG, did he really offer me food? Is it that obvious I am famished? I felt like I had won the jackpot.

"Lucas, I would love anything to eat and a water," I said confidently, knowing I had no right to ask.

"No problem," he said and turned on his heels and disappeared into the store. About ten minutes later, Lucas exited the store and walked over to my table. "Here you go, Liz," he said as he placed the spoils on the table before me.

I couldn't believe what he had purchased: a turkey sandwich, potato chips, an apple, a chocolate chip cookie, and a large water, more food than I had eaten in the last week!

"Oh my gosh, Lucas, you are too generous! Thank you so much," I exclaimed as I began to tear up.

"Happy to do it," he said.

Eventually, the boys got restless and decided to move on to their next destination. Lucas led the goodbyes and shouted to me, "Nice to meet you, Liz!"

The group of boys followed in unison waving goodbye, and off they went. Now that my belly was full, I turned my attention to my feet. Still barefoot and dirty as can be from the hospital roof, I looked at the bloody blisters and wondered what to do. I had seen a pharmacy in a building near the hospital and thought maybe I could get help there for my feet. I decided to leave the convenience store and walk to the pharmacy.

Chapter 39

The Pharmacy

Along the way to the pharmacy, I encountered Roger at a different bus stop. As I approached, he turned to me and smiled brightly.

"Hey, Liz! I was hoping I would run into you again," he said.

"Me too! How is your dad doing?" I asked.

"He's okay. Surgery is done, but he hasn't woken up yet," he replied.

"I'm sure he will be fine soon," I said, knowing full well that I had no idea how he would fare.

"What are you up to now, Liz?" Roger asked.

I told him I was going to look for some bandages at the pharmacy for my feet.

"Where are your shoes, Liz?" he asked.

"I don't have any," I blurted.

Don't have any? What the hell was I saying? I had over fifty pairs of shoes. I just had no idea where they were and why I was here without even a single pair. I would have settled for four-inch-high heels at that point. I glanced again at Roger's fancy, shiny shoes and wondered how much they must have cost. *Who was this dude, and why was he trying to give the impression that he was homeless?*

"Here, take these," Roger said as he tossed a pair of new socks at me.

"What's this?" I asked.

"I got you a pair of socks," he replied.

"You did?" I asked incredulously. "Why?"

"Because I like you. I like your spunk," he said.

I sat back down and quickly put the socks on, pulling them up over my bloody feet, smiling at the Pokémon theme. "I'm a Pokémon! Thank you so much!" I shouted as I stood to my feet and began to walk to the pharmacy. I looked back and saw Roger smiling and waving at me.

"See you later, I hope," he said.

As I neared the office building adjacent to the hospital, I noticed an "Open" sign on the window of the pharmacy. I walked into the foyer of the building and noticed the fancy décor: a beautiful, light-filled atrium with a large water feature and high-end furnishings with dramatic artwork. *This is no ordinary medical office building*, I thought. The building was named after Ronald Reagan, so I assumed I must be in the Simi Valley of north Los Angeles, where many things are named after this former president. There is no easy way to get there without a car. *How the hell did I get here?* I wondered.

Simi Valley is an affluent suburb in Southern California, and the parking lot of the building did not disappoint, with row after row of parked luxury vehicles with chauffeur-driven Rolls-Royces waiting at the curb.

From the fancy atrium, I took a sharp left and entered the pharmacy. It smelled like an old compounding pharmacy. There were a few shelves of products and a typical window to interact with the pharmacists. I scoured the shelves for anything to help with my feet. The selection was limited because it was such a small pharmacy. I perused the shelves and gathered a few staples: Band-Aids, Ace wraps, antibiotic ointment, and silicone for my blisters. There were no prices on the items or the shelves. I had no idea how much my armful of first-aid goodies would cost, and I had no ability to pay.

Holding the array of products in my arms, I began to panic, so I decided to put the items back on the shelf and take a little time to think about what to do. I briefly considered stealing a thing or two, but fortunately thought the better of that idea. I still had a Rolex on, and I thought maybe I could use that for collateral until I could return with money. No idea seemed very good, so I decided to take a walk around the building and think about my options for a little while.

My feet felt much better in the Pokémon socks as I walked along the scorched sidewalk. How could I ever thank Roger for them?

I found a bench under a tree off the building's parking lot and took a seat. I tried to quiet my mind and think of a solution for procuring first-aid items. Finally, a brilliant idea came to me. I walked back to the pharmacy and gathered back all the items I had previously picked out. I confidently took them to the pharmacy register to check out. I placed the items on the counter and waited for assistance.

It wasn't long before a young woman approached me. "Did you find everything today?"

"Yes, I think I did." I watched nervously as she rang up each item. The cash register was old and slow, and I was unable to see the prices and anxiously awaited the tally.

"That will be seventy-five dollars," she said.

Holy crap, I thought. *This place is expensive!*

"I'd like to put these on my account," I said confidently to the cashier.

"Sure, what is the name on the account?" she asked.

"Liz Reagan," I instinctively replied. *This is Reagan Town*, I thought to myself.

"No problem. Here you go, Liz," she replied and handed me a white bag with items in it after I signed the receipt.

"Thank you very much," I said and quickly exited the building.

Chapter 40
The Conundrum

I returned to the bus stop and searched for Roger. He was nowhere to be found. I sat down on the bench and removed the Pokémon socks from my feet and laid them next to me. I opened the pharmacy bag and realized that in my haste, nervousness, and fuzzy thinking, I must have mistakenly picked an assortment of unrelated items from the pharmacy: no Band- Aids, no Ace wrap, and so forth. Instead, I was left with an assortment of hair ties, Vaseline, and a pair of cheap costume jewelry earrings. A bunch of useless items and nothing to nurse my feet back to health.

I put the dirty socks back on, put on the pair of tacky, plastic earrings, and waited. In hindsight, I now wonder if the cashier purposely put those erroneous items in my bag rather than the expensive first-aid items. Thank God she was at least kind to me in what could have been a very sticky situation.

The sun was starting to set, and for the first time all day, I gave thought to my future. As the sun set and darkness took over, I began to panic. I had been in pretty much the same place all day and hadn't figured out exactly where I was or where I was going. I knew I needed to get to my Airbnb many miles away in West Los Angeles but had no idea how I would do that. My ride-share app was on my absent phone, my credit cards and cash were gone, and I didn't know my own address at the Airbnb. *I am fucked. Will I sleep on the street? Will someone take me in? What am I going to do?*

The bus stop at that time of day was busy with lots of people coming and going. I sat and watched people for a while and thought about striking up a conversation with someone, someone who looked nice and non-threatening. I searched for such a person, including the kind gentleman who gave me cash earlier in the day, but didn't feel confident enough to approach anyone.

Suddenly, I felt naked and afraid. I was sure that everyone could see through me to my disoriented core. But, alas, no one paid me a minute of attention or asked if I needed help, and I was too ashamed to ask or be honest with anyone. I was, however, lucid enough to bite my tongue and stay quiet, so I didn't end up in the hospital or jail.

As darkness descended, my anxiety heightened. *What the hell am I going to do?* I kept asking myself.

I tried so hard to rack my brain for the reason I was in this town north of Los Angeles. *Was I supposed to have a meeting here with someone?* I did know a guy who worked in Simi Valley, an attorney I had worked with previously, but did not recall setting an appointment with him.

I looked all around the bus stop as far as I could see. A cop drove right past me, but I didn't have the courage to ask him to stop and help me. What would I even tell him? "Hi, my name is Liz. I have no idea why I am here in your town, and I don't remember my address where I am staying in Los Angeles."

It didn't seem like a winning approach, so I sat motionless on the bus stop bench.

Chapter 41

The Hospital, Again

Directly ahead of me was the hospital. I stared at it for a long time as the streetlights above me turned on and the stars began to appear. The traffic died down, and soon I found myself alone at the bus stop. I search anxiously for Roger. *Where was he? Didn't he tell me he would be back to meet me at the stop?* I really couldn't remember, and I felt it was getting too late to stay out in the darkness. I decided to go to the hospital.

I jaywalked across the street and entered the lobby of the hospital. I smiled at the similarity to the hospital I had worked in for years. It felt familiar, and I instantly felt safer. I approached the reception desk and said to the young man behind the counter, "Hi. I need help."

"How can I help?" he asked.

"I need to call for a taxi, but I don't have a phone," I said.

He replied, "I don't think we even have taxis in this town anymore. Just Lyft or Uber."

I told him I could only take an old-school taxi because I would need to pay for the ride when I reached my destination, not on an app.

"Oh, I see," he said. "Let me see what I can do."

He left the desk and disappeared for a few minutes. I looked around me and saw several groups of families set to visit their loved ones in the hospital. I hoped I might see Roger in the lobby, but he was nowhere to be found.

The young man returned to the desk and said, "I called a taxi. They will be here soon."

"Oh my gosh, thank you so much," I said.

"No problem," he replied. "Help yourself to coffee or tea," he said while pointing to a self-serve coffee bar in the hospital lobby.

Coffee at nine o'clock at night? I thought. *Sure! Who knows how long I will be up tonight?* I quickly poured a cup of coffee and put in massive amounts of sugar and cream. *This will have to suffice for dinner,* I said to myself.

I took my sorry ass over to a bank of chairs in the lobby to wait for the taxi. I collapsed into the chair, now knowing I would be on my way back to Los Angeles soon. I was hungry, super hungry. I looked down at my arms and legs and marveled at how skinny they were. I had had body dysmorphia since I was a child, and this newfound extreme thinness was very pleasing to me. It seemed to please others, too, in the appearance-obsessed city of Los Angeles. *You truly can't be too rich or too thin in this town,* I thought.

Although it was only about a thirty-minute wait, it seemed like an eternity. Finally, I saw the familiar taxi sign pull up on top of a small car. I walked out of the hospital in my new socks and opened the car door.

"Where are you headed to?" the driver asked.

"Los Angeles," I replied.

"Where in Los Angeles?" he asked.

"West Los Angeles," I replied.

"I'm not going anywhere near Los Angeles, lady," he said as he inched the car forward.

"What? Are you kidding me?" I asked. "Why not?"

"Because it's too far away," he said as he began to drive away. I slammed the moving car door and turned on my heel and went back into the hospital.

"What happened?" the young man at the desk asked.

"He wouldn't take me to Los Angeles," I answered. Now, I was really getting worried about how I was going to get back to the apartment.

"Let me try again," he said and disappeared behind an "employees only" door.

After a few minutes, the very helpful young man returned and let me know he had called for another taxi. "This time, I told them you are going to West Los Angeles. They reassured me that this driver was cool with that."

Chapter 42

Back to Los Angeles

A few minutes later, a second taxi rounded the corner and pulled up under the porte cochere. This time, I leaned through the front window and made sure he would take me to my destination before getting in.

"Yes, I take you there," he said in broken English while motioning to me to get in the car. He was wearing a Punjabi and appeared to be sincere. I hesitated for a nanosecond and then hopped in the car.

"Where are you going in Los Angeles?" he asked.

"I'll be able to take you there, but I don't know the address," I said, hoping I was right.

"Do you want me to take the 101 to the 405?" he asked.

I searched the battered hard drive in my brain for any recognition of an address, but none was forthcoming.

"Yes, that should be good," I said. "Once we pass the Getty, I'll be able to direct you to the place I am staying."

Traffic was still formidable at this late hour. Really, the only time I have found the Los Angeles freeways to be somewhat empty is from 3:00 a.m. to 4:00 a.m. At 10:00 p.m., as it was now, a steady stream of cars was racing into the city.

Sitting in the back of the junker taxi, I watched as fancy cars flew by me up over the 405 and down into the city: Lamborghinis, Aston Martins, Rolls-Royce, Bentleys, Ferraris, and more. In this town, it is impossible to stand out in the usual luxury cars of my hometown. Mercedes, Porsche, and BMW were all too banal for Los Angeles. I smiled at the thought that my $150,000 Mercedes was a car for commoners and soccer moms here. *Only in Southern California*, I thought.

After an hour of driving, we pulled into the parking lot of the apartment complex where I was staying.

"I have to run upstairs to get my wallet," I said as he parked.

"What? That's not okay," he answered.

"Sir, I don't have a choice. My money is upstairs in an apartment," I replied.

"I see you have a fancy watch there," he stated, looking at my gold Rolex.

"Here, keep this as collateral while I go get cash," I said as I took off my watch and handed it to him. "This ought to be more than enough to cover the ride if I don't come back," I said as I exited the car.

What the hell have I just done? I left a $20,000 watch with a stranger to cover a $200 taxi fare. I sure hope he doesn't leave! I said to myself as I climbed the stairs to the apartment door.

Once at the apartment entrance, I realized I didn't have my key, and the door was dead-bolted shut. I had no recollection of ever leaving the apartment for the day I had in the Valley. I paced frantically in front of the doorway and berated myself for the situation I was in. I had to get in some way, somehow.

I walked around the perimeter of the apartment as best I could and strategized a way in. I surmised I needed to do some acrobatics to hoist myself up over a wall and onto one of the balconies. I jumped the wall, crawled myself up and over the barricade, and landed on my ass on the deck of the apartment. I placed my hand on the door handle of the sliding glass door and was ecstatic to find that the door was unlocked.

"Whew," I shouted once inside, instantly grateful I had been so sloppy.

The apartment was a mess, and I had no idea where my wallet was. Rather than taking the time to find it, I went to my secret stash of cash and took out three crisp $100 bills. Although the taxi ride was only $200, it seemed appropriate to tip the driver 50 percent.

I weaved my way from the apartment back to the parking lot where the driver was still waiting.

"Liz!" he exclaimed. "You came back!"

"Of course I did," I said as I handed him the crisp bills.

"Wow!" he said as he quickly counted the cash. "Here, I can't accept all this, Liz. I was only doing my job." He thrust a $100 bill back at me.

Given it was now nearly 11:00 p.m. and I was exhausted, I didn't put up a fuss and took the money back from him.

"Here's my card in case you need another ride in the future," he said as he handed me his business card and my Rolex. I smiled as I read it, "Navi: I'll drive you anywhere but crazy." I saw a phone number listed below.

"Thanks a lot, Navi," I said as I turned away and walked back to the apartment.

Chapter 43
Nighttime Escapades

I headed back and entered the apartment through the front door this time. I could smell the remains of my neighbors' dinner wafting through the apartment breezeway and realized how hungry I was. My clothes, which fit snugly just a few months ago, now hung on me like I was a hanger. Bones protruded out beneath my clothes, and for the first time in my life, my arm veins were visible. *It looks like I'm a gym rat*, I thought to myself as I headed to the kitchen, taking delight in my new physique and the fact I hadn't had to hit the gym.

Once in the kitchen, I took in the sight: dirty dishes stacked to the height of the upper cabinets, food spoiling on the counter, mold everywhere, and an empty fridge. *Not very appetizing*, I thought, but I was not distressed at the condition of the kitchen. Clearly, I had caused the mess, but I had no recollection of doing so, and I couldn't remember the last time I was in the apartment. *Hmmmm*, I pondered. *What to do now?*

I decided to head out to the streets of Santa Monica on foot at 11:30 p.m. to find some food. Los Angeles was definitely not New York City, a place I had once lived, with the 24/7 availability of anything you wanted. I was hopeful, however, that there would be something for me to eat at that hour.

Before I left the apartment, I made sure to freshen up, applying a little makeup, fixing my hair, and changing my clothes. This time, I put on comfy UGGS after applying a few Band-Aids to my weary feet.

I walked the long, windy path out of the apartment complex, brushing past lush foliage of palm trees and bougainvillea, and exited the locked, iron gate to the street. I was staying just a couple blocks from Santa Monica Boulevard, and I knew the streets well. I walked quickly past the dark and foreboding entrance to the Veterans Medical Center. I smiled at the memory of my recent escapades there that had resulted in a few new friends and a pair of green army combat boots, given to me by an Iraq war veteran Charlie.

I rounded the corner and walked toward the hustle and bustle of Santa Monica Boulevard. Cars full of loud, partying kids zoomed past me as I sat down at a bus stop to rest. One aspect of all this weight loss and boundless energy was that I tired easily. I assumed it was from the weight loss, but I was all too happy with my physique to investigate it further. I thought it was incredibly cool that I could eat anything I wanted and still lose weight. Earlier in my life, I had stated if I was ever in that state, "Take me to the hospital," meaning "something is wrong." But presently, I wasn't worried.

After a few minutes at the bus stop, I turned around to see a man walking toward me. While I didn't recognize him specifically, I remembered him as someone who hung out with a group of homeless people in this hood.

"Hi, Liz!" he said as he approached.

"Hi," I said back, amused he knew my name, not remembering having met him before.

"What are you doing here this time of night?" he asked sincerely.

"I just got back into town [a true story], and I am hungry," I replied. "It looks like Subway is all that is open right now."

"Hey, do you like Mexican food?" he asked.

"I absolutely love Mexican food," I replied.

"Here, come with me. I know the best food in town," he said as he gently grabbed my elbow to help me up from the bench.

"I'm so sorry. I don't recall your name," I said as we walked down the street together.

"My name is Jimmy, Liz," he answered.

"Of course, Jimmy," I said. "Sorry about that. It's been a very long day."

If he only knew, I thought to myself.

We walked side by side for a few blocks, past all the shops I had come to know in recent times: dry cleaners, bank, convenience store, gas station, art store, and more. I was surprised when Jimmy switched sides with me and placed himself on the roadside side of the sidewalk, a nod to chivalry that was pretty much a thing of the past. Who was this dude? And why did I trust him?

As we continued to walk down Santa Monica Boulevard toward the ocean, I saw a food truck ahead with a throng of people surrounding it.

"This is the best Mexican food in Los Angeles," Jimmy proclaimed as he motioned to the food truck. "These guys lost their lease downtown, so they bought a truck, and here they are!" he exclaimed excitedly. "Hey, Liz! Do you have any money? I'm all out," he stated as we approached the truck.

"This is my treat, Jimmy," I replied, grateful for the company.

There was a long line, and it didn't appear to be moving fast. I was very hungry at this point and couldn't wait to eat.

"Jimmy, can you please order for me?" I asked. "And don't forget, I'm really hungry!"

"Me, too!" he said as we inched toward the front of the line.

I stepped aside from the line and lit a cigarette. I looked around me to see men and women of all ages huddled together, waiting for their food. Most of the conversations were in Spanish, so all I could really do was smile at everyone around me. I heard Jimmy order what sounded like enough food for an army and couldn't wait to eat.

Jimmy ordered our food in Spanish, and I paid the bill of $25. We took our food over to a parking lot and sat on the curb as we ate.

"Hey, Liz, do you want a beer?" Jimmy asked.

"I would love one!" I replied as I pulled out a $10 bill from my purse and handed it to him. I knew it was useless to expect him to pay.

Jimmy hopped up and nearly ran to a nearby convenience store, returning with two Coors Light. If only he knew that this was my least favorite beer of all time.

"Thank you, Jimmy," I said as I took one of the cans from him.

Jimmy ate fast and gulped down the beer before I had even made a dent in my food.

"Hey, Liz, I need to go now. I've got friends waiting for me over on Wilshire Boulevard," he said as he crumpled up the food wrappings and smashed the empty can.

"No problem, Jimmy," I said as he walked away. I didn't know if I would ever see him again, but I didn't really mind that possibility either.

After I finished my food and beer, I walked back to the apartment and fell fast asleep.

Chapter 44
Leaving for Las Vegas

I woke up the next morning after a solid twelve-hour sleep devoid of dreams or interruptions. I made a cup of coffee and drank it with a cigarette out on the balcony, marveling at the deep blue sky and the sounds of tropical birds. Life seemed peaceful and hopeful at that moment. I had pretty much forgotten about the escapades from the previous day and night and got on my computer to do some work for my business in Seattle. My head seemed clearer and gone for the moment were the delusions and hallucinations that had become so familiar. I decided it was time to reconsider my future.

I had visited Los Angeles enough to know that if I were going to be financially successful, I probably needed to consider moving to a more tax-advantaged state than California. Given that Nevada was close to where I was visiting in California, I impulsively decided to drive the G-Wagon to Las Vegas to check it out.

After a few days at the apartment, I woke up one morning on a flawless, sunny day and decided it was time to check out Las Vegas.

I knew the drive through the desert would be very hot, so I packed lots of bottles of water with me. I didn't know where I was going or where I was going to stay or for how long, so I packed my large suitcase with most of my worldly possessions with me in California, including my cash. I dressed in white ripped jeans, beige UGGs, a white lace cami, and a white leather jacket. Of course, I didn't forget the bling and brought all the jewelry I had with me in Los Angeles for the trip to Las Vegas.

I pulled out from the apartment complex and drove a short distance to the 405. I headed south until I hit the 10 and then turned east for the long drive. I had forgotten to eat breakfast and decided I would stop along the way.

A couple hours later, about halfway to Las Vegas, I found a classic diner in the middle of nowhere. As I pulled off the exit, I noticed I needed gas. I pulled into a gas station conveniently located next to the diner. But as I approached the pumps, I noticed that every lane was blocked off with orange cones, indicating no gas.

"What the hell?" I said out loud. It was clear that I was not going to get any gas there. As it was the only station for miles, I decided to go look for gas after breakfast.

I parked the car in a dusty, unmarked lot adjacent to the diner. I was starting to get used to the excessive heat and its impact on the contents of a car. I didn't want to fry everything I had packed, so I wheeled my huge suitcase with me into the restaurant. I stood at the hostess station for a few minutes until a crusty old woman in an apron approached me.

"Table for two?" she asked, pointing to my suitcase and me.

"Hilarious," I replied. "No, it's just me."

"You can leave your suitcase up here," she said, motioning to the hostess stand.

"No thanks," I said, "I'll keep it with me." I didn't want to risk losing all my worldly possessions.

I followed the hostess to a four-top table in the middle of the large dining room, bummed that I couldn't sit at a booth. I walked past table after table of jovial people eating what looked to be very good food. I could feel their stares as I walked past each table and wondered what they were thinking about me.

Do they know who I am? Of course not, Liz. Were they headed to Las Vegas like I was? Maybe. It all seemed very exciting at that moment, and I couldn't wait to have breakfast.

I felt self-conscious eating alone that day. Normally, it doesn't bother me at all to eat alone, as I have done all over the world when traveling for business. But on this day, I felt uncomfortable and out of place. To be honest, I was quite lonely at that time in my life and longed to be one of the people near me who were part of a group. I perused the menu and finally decided on a vegetarian omelet.

"Would you like hash browns or house potatoes?" the waitress asked.

"Neither, thank you," I said quietly.

"How many pancakes would you like? The omelet comes with up to three buttermilk pancakes," she continued.

"I'll have one," I acquiesced. For most of my adult life, I had been on a keto-type of diet and was not used to ordering carbs. Now, however, I had lost so much weight that I figured a little pancake couldn't hurt me.

I nursed a cup of coffee while I waited for my food. I tried to look entertained and busy by staring at my phone. I hadn't had much communication with Steve Jobs during this most recent visit to Southern California, so I decided to get on the internet and see what I could find.

I searched Google by putting in the search term, "What do I need to know today?" This had worked for me in the past, granting me access to exclusive content curated by Steve for me. Today, however, I drew a blank screen when I searched the phrase. I quickly checked my internet connection, and all seemed to be copacetic.

Why can't I get on the internet? I wondered. *No matter.* As I was struggling with my phone, my food arrived.

"Here you go, young lady," the waitress said.

I was amused, as I believed I was much older than she was, but we had clearly lived two very different lives: she with bronzed, sun-damaged skin and premature wrinkles; and me with my sun-free, wrinkle-free skin.

I perused the food in front of me, truly enough for three of me. Although I was famished, I only ate half of the omelet and a few bites of the pancake.

"May I please have a box?" I asked the busboy.

"Absolutely," he said and quickly retrieved one for me.

I loaded up my food into the Styrofoam to-go container and headed for the exit with my suitcase.

"That will be eleven dollars," the cashier said to me.

"Eleven dollars total?" I asked incredulously.

That is ridiculous! That wouldn't even buy you a piece of avocado toast in Los Angeles! I thought.

I handed her a crisp $20 bill and said, "Thank you!"

"Wait! Don't you want your change?" she shouted at me as I pushed open the door to the parking lot.

"Nope! Keep it! Thank you!" I said as the glass door shut behind me and I dragged my suitcase to the scorching car.

Chapter 45
On the Road Again

I loaded my suitcase back into the car and drove past the gas station one more time before I got back on the freeway. *Still closed,* I thought to myself as I checked the gas gauge. *A quarter tank left and a long way to drive to get to Las Vegas.* I hoped there would be another gas station before I ran out of gas.

I turned on my favorite music, took off my shoes, and turned up the air-conditioning. My car told me it was ninety-eight degrees outside already on this cloudless morning, and I knew it was going to be a hot one as I traversed the desert.

As I reached a cruising speed of seventy-five miles per hour on the highway to Vegas, my car's navigation spontaneously started and asked if I wanted it to take over. Given that I didn't have a specific destination, I pushed the yes button confidently and was excited and relieved to see where it would take me this time. It let me know that there was a gas station ahead and that I should stop there for gas.

As I pulled off the freeway about fifty miles east of the diner, I realized that my gas light had been on for quite a while. My car told me I was on reserve fuel, so I was thrilled to find an open station. As is customary at rest stops, I got out of the car to stretch my legs a bit while waiting.

I walked away from the gas pumps and my refueling car and headed to a grassy area with picnic tables and lots of people milling around. I stood on the sidelines watching the people and pets and was jolted back to reality when a young couple approached me.

"Hi! We are Jake and Melissa. What's your name?" the girl asked timidly.

"Hi. I'm Liz." I noticed that they seemed very young and a bit out of place. "What are you guys up to?"

"We were on our way to Las Vegas from Los Angeles when our rig broke down," Jake replied as he motioned toward an old Airstream parked alongside the gas station.

"What's wrong with it?" I asked.

"It's the water pump, they think," Melissa answered.

"Do you guys need a ride to Vegas?" I asked.

"They are going to tell us soon if they can fix our vehicle," Jake replied.

"I can't wait too long, but if you need a ride, I can take you," I finished.

Jake, Melissa, and I stood around in a circle and shared cigarettes and brief stories of our lives. They were both actors from Los Angeles moving to Las Vegas to create a new life for themselves. They had fallen on hard times in California and were living in their mobile home, moving from neighborhood to neighborhood, always outrunning the authorities. Jake had lost his day job after being diagnosed with bipolar disorder, and Melissa suffered from a devastating autoimmune disease. They both seemed on the edge, and I felt their pain. I didn't share much of my own drama, as it didn't really seem necessary. I wished that there was some way I could help, but I came up with no solutions.

I waited for about fifteen minutes and then let them know I had to leave.

"No problem, Liz. Thanks for the offer," Jake said.

I felt a bit sheepish leaving them at the rest stop, but I didn't apparently feel they needed saving at that moment. Steve had not let me know that I should try to save these two, so I didn't push it. I did take $500 cash out of my stash and handed it to Jake before driving away.

"I'm sorry I can't do more for you at this time," I said as I watched him finger the bills as his mouth opened in disbelief.

"Liz, we just met you!" Jake replied.

"Happy to help. Maybe we will see each other in Vegas!" I finished as I began to drive away.

I got back on the freeway, and as Los Angeles faded behind me, the energy of Las Vegas welcomed me with open arms. I followed the GPS and drove slowly through the heart of town. I had been there many, many times over the years, but never as a potential resident driving my own car.

The car took me down the Strip past all the usual haunts. I inched along in traffic, going about fifteen miles per hour, which allowed me to take in the sights: Wynn, Aria, Caesar's Palace, MGM Grand, Paris, New York, and more. I played Coldplay loudly with my windows down and sang along, imagining what it would be like to live in this town. It felt much more familiar than Los Angeles, but it still wasn't home. I wondered where my car was taking me.

Chapter 46
Hotel Las Vegas

I had spent time in Las Vegas at numerous medical conferences held on the Strip, and I didn't know much about the city or how it would be living there. About a decade previously, I had purchased a timeshare in Las Vegas but had never set foot on the property, using it only for its trading power.

The frank truth is I was in no condition at that time to evaluate such a move to Las Vegas, and the city is anything but welcoming for those who are suffering. Las Vegas city caters to high rollers and the vast population of tourists, but for the unstable visitor or resident, it can become a scary, unwelcoming place, in my experience.

The car's GPS took me off the Strip and toward a part of town I hadn't been to before. I drove slowly as I approached my destination per the car: Trump Tower Las Vegas. I had never been to this hotel before, but I knew it did not have gambling, which made me happy.

I pulled the G-Wag up to the bell desk under the ornate porte cochere. Lavish gold, chrome, crystal, and marble all coalesced to produce a grand entrance fit for a queen. One of the many uniformed bellhops came to my door and waited for me to indicate I was getting out.

"Welcome to Trump Tower! Are you staying with us, miss?" the handsome bellhop asked.

"Yes, I hope so. I need to see if there is an available room," I said confidently.

"Awesome. I'll move your car over there while you check in," he replied.

There were limos everywhere around me, and I half-wondered if Mr. Trump himself were there. *Of course not, Liz*, I said to myself.

I had a brush with Mr. Trump in the 1980s at Trump Tower while living in New York City. Ever since then, I had been a fan of his drive and passion for all things luxurious. Staying at this property seemed like a perfect resting ground for my weary body and soul.

I approached the front desk and waited for one of the impossibly good-looking and impeccably dressed front desk staff to motion to me to approach the desk.

"Hello! Checking in?" the young woman asked.

"I hope so," I responded to her. "What do you have available?"

"Let me check," she said. "How long will you be staying with us?"

I truly had no idea how to answer that question. "Forever?" I replied as I smiled and looked around the incredible foyer.

It was a sight to behold. So much beauty and opulence all at once. I felt at home there, I truly did, and did not want to leave, ever. I had stayed at Wynn many times before, among other hotels on the Strip, and I felt like Trump Tower was the most beautiful of all. I braced myself for the answer from the clerk, believing I may not want to afford this hotel.

"I only have a suite available," the woman said.

I steeled myself for the cost and asked, "What is the best price you can give me on that suite?"

"One hundred and fifty dollars a night," she replied.

Seriously? How could that be? Other luxury hotels on the Strip cost three times as much.

"I hate to ask, but how much is your parking?" I asked in reply. I had encountered hotels in Las Vegas that charge upward of $70 per day to park a vehicle.

"Parking is complimentary," she replied.

Now I truly knew I had found my home away from home. "Wonderful," I said. "I'll take it! Do you take cash?"

"Yes, we do take cash," the beautiful girl said to me with a grin that said, "No duh, lady."

I grabbed my satchel of cash off my shoulder and placed it on the counter in front of me. I had brought nearly $100,000 cash with me and felt a little uncomfortable with it. The receptionist saw my loot and said, "Miss, would you like to store your cash in our vault?"

"That would be incredible," I replied.

She then pulled her walkie-talkie from her waistline and spoke into it. "Would management please come to the front desk?"

It only took a few minutes before a sharply dressed, dapper, older man approached us and greeted me. "Hello, miss. I understand you would like to put something in the vault?"

"Yes, I would," I replied.

"Follow me, please," he said as he walked around the desk toward me.

We walked from the lobby past the gift shop and entered through a door labeled "Private." We weaved our way through the back of the house until we reached the vault.

It looked to me like the kind of vault you would see at a bank. An armed guard was standing outside the vault door, who remained expressionless as we walked past him. The vault was large, and I could only imagine the spoils that must reside within the thick, steel walls.

"This will be yours for the duration of your stay," the manager said as he motioned to an open door in the vault wall, number thirty-six. The cubby was generous in size and easily held my cash. "You will have 24/7 access to this vault, so feel free to put anything you want in it." He shut and locked the door to my cubby, holding all my money and handed me the key. "Very glad to have you stay with us, miss."

"The pleasure is all mine," I replied and followed him out of the vault.

I reentered the lobby and smiled at the front desk staff as I walked toward the bell desk. I searched for the bellhop who had helped me previously, but couldn't find him anywhere. I approached the bell desk, and an energetic young man offered me a bottle of water. I hadn't really noticed the heat, but now I realized I was parched.

"Thank you!" I gratefully took the bottle and finished it all at once.

"You can come to us and get water any time you want," he said as he handed me another bottle.

"That's awesome. Thank you," I replied. "I need to get my luggage brought up to my room," I said to him as I gestured to my car, still under the porte cochere.

"That's an awesome car!" the man said as he grabbed my keys and ran over to it to get my luggage. "I'll meet you in your room," the bellhop shouted.

I turned around and walked back into the ornate lobby. "Wow," I said under my breath. "This place is awesome." I walked through the elegant hallway and to the elevators after an armed guard checked my ID and room key.

This is some major security, I thought to myself as I boarded the elevator. I looked at my room key and pressed the "PH" button. *How on earth did I score a penthouse suite for $150 a night?* I wondered. This lucky break only served to make my resolve to move to Las Vegas fiercer. I liked it there, or so I thought.

Chapter 47
The Las Vegas Suite

I exited the elevator and walked down a long hallway to the end. There were two suites, and one of them was mine. I gingerly opened the door and slowly went in. *Holy sheesh,* I thought as I viewed the floor-to-ceiling windows overlooking the Las Vegas Strip and all its glory.

The opulence of the suite was extreme and somewhat overwhelming. I had a full kitchen, dining room, separate bedroom, and a bathroom the size of my former apartment in New York City. I took a quick tour around the place and figured I had about one thousand square feet. As I passed the front door, I heard a gentle knock and the familiar greeting of a bellhop delivering luggage.

I opened the door and let in the bellhop. He had a cart piled high with everything from my car. I realized I had forgotten to tell him, "Just bring up the suitcase," so he had emptied everything and brought it up. I was too embarrassed to let him know I only needed the suitcase and began to help him unload everything.

"Would you like me to unpack your luggage, miss?" he asked.

"No, thank you. I've got it," I said.

The bellhop had brought a large box with him that wasn't mine, and as he was leaving, he emptied the contents on the dining room table. "Here you go, miss," he said as he placed a chilled bottle of champagne, ice bucket, and glasses onto the table and placed numerous bottles of water in the fridge.

"I didn't order anything, sir," I said.

"Compliments of the house," he said as he headed toward the door.

"Oh, wait! Don't forget this," I said as I handed him a crisp $100 bill into his hand. He looked at what I had given him and, without blinking an eye, said, "I'm happy to help anytime. Just call the bell desk and ask for me. My name is Aaron."

"Thank you so much, Aaron. I'll be sure to call on you when needed," I replied.

After Aaron left, I collapsed onto the bed and stared out the window. *What am I doing here? Where am I going?* I had left Los Angeles in search of a better tax structure but had no new income to worry about sheltering anyway! All I had been doing was spending money, without anything to show for it.

The billion-dollar company I had been working to form had pretty much collapsed in the weeks prior to my visit to Las Vegas. My mood had become erratic, and my mind raced 24/7. The flow of creative ideas would not stop, and I would annoy my family, friends, and employees at all hours of the day and night with frenzied calls, emails, texts, thoughts, and ideas for all my companies.

Over the previous couple of years, everything had seemed to be a good idea to pursue, including new businesses, new friendships, new relationships, new locales, and more. I had been working at an untenable pace for decades, and now suddenly felt that everything was catching up to me. I looked forward to taking a much-needed break in Nevada.

Before I had left Los Angeles for Las Vegas, I'd had another major falling out with my oldest son, which only got worse each time we saw each other in Los Angeles. He had always been there for me over the years, and I was there for him. But his college years in Los Angeles had put a distance between us that continued long after his graduation. Even though there was no objective evidence, I believed he was actively trying to ruin me and did my best to avoid him at all costs whenever I visited California.

Now that I was staying in Las Vegas, I felt protected from his presence and all the trauma/drama we had been through recently. While still thinking about my son, I fell fast asleep on the bed for a couple of hours.

Chapter 48
Chillin' in Las Vegas

I woke up with a start and was completely disoriented. I looked out the window, realized where I was, and sighed a sigh of relief when I realized I was in Nevada, not California.

I got up, grabbed a water out of the fridge, and decided to go visit the pool and check out the cabanas. I quickly changed into my new swimsuit, fancy cover-up, Dior sunglasses, and broad-rimmed, floppy hat. Complete with designer rhinestone flip-flops, I looked like the part of a Las Vegas pool party guest. I opened the champagne and poured a glass into my Mercedes to-go coffee cup and headed to the sun deck.

Once at the pool, I looked around and saw the cabanas at one end of the facility. I noticed that most of the cabanas were empty, while the lounge chairs were all full. As I didn't want to sit in the direct sun anyway, always worried about my skin, I approached the nearest pool attendant and inquired about the cabana.

"May I sit in here?" I asked while gesturing to the nearest cabana.

"Yes, absolutely," she replied.

"Wonderful. I'll take this one," I said as I walked into the oversized cabana, complete with a stocked fridge, fresh fruit plate, crunchy snacks, and more. "Is there a charge?" I asked after sitting down on one of the overstuffed, comfortable couches.

"Yes, $200 per day," the attendant answered.

Excuse me? $200? More than my suite? I thought to myself.

"Okay," I replied, "please charge it to room 2208." I handed her my room key, cracked open a seltzer, and helped myself to some fruit.

Even though I was resting in the cabana, it was still scorching hot. The attendant came back in, almost as if on cue, and turned on a portable air-conditioner.

"That's awesome!" I exclaimed, having never seen an air-conditioner in a cabana before.

"Please let me know if you need anything else, miss," she said.

I could get used to this life, I thought as she left. The air-conditioner helped quite a bit, and I realized I was hungry again. I hadn't eaten much at the diner, and I had been too busy to think about food since arriving in Las Vegas. I told myself it must be my inattention to food that was causing my rapid weight loss.

I looked around the cabana and found a food menu near the television. I turned on Fox News first and flipped the channel back and forth from Fox to CNN. The namesake of the hotel I was staying in was the President of the United States at that time, and I felt it my duty to keep up to date on him while staying in his palace. I perused the menu and decided on a Cobb salad and another glass of bubbly. I gave my order to the attendant and watched Anderson Cooper until the food came.

A short time later, a server walked toward me in the cabana with the requisite tray on his arm. He entered the cabana and placed the tray on the coffee table before me. I hadn't known what to expect, but the food and service did not disappoint. Linens, silver, impeccable salad, and a basket of breads/crackers/butter. It was enough food for a couple of meals, but I was so hungry that I nearly ate everything in front of me.

"All finished?" the attendant asked me.

"Yes, thank you so much," I replied. "Say, is there a spa here?"

"Yes, we have a full-service spa open every day of the week," she said. "Would you like me to make a reservation for you?"

"That would be great! I would like a manicure and a pedicure, please," I replied.

She disappeared for a few minutes and came back and said, "You're all set for 10:00 a.m. tomorrow morning."

I thanked her and decided to leave the cabana after letting my food digest a bit.

As I walked back up to my room, I realized just how exhausted I was. In the previous weeks, my nerves had been burned to crisps, and my neurons seemed to fire inexplicably and without a fire extinguisher. I couldn't remember the last time I had felt at peace. And here, I had found with the help of my magic car, nirvana at Trump Tower Las

Vegas. I felt like I could have gone to sleep for years, waking up like Rip Van Winkle.

I entered my suite and noticed a huge, beautiful bouquet of flowers on the dining table where the champagne had been. "Where did you come from?" I asked the flowers.

Surprisingly, they didn't reply. I searched my brain for any potential secret (or not-so-secret) admirer and came up empty-handed. I figured someone would eventually spill the beans. Until then, I decided to enjoy them after picking out the lilies. Anyone who knew me well would know I am terribly allergic to the stamen of lilies. The rest of the flowers that remained still left a beautiful sight.

I unpacked my huge suitcase of its contents into the massive, opulent bureau in the bedroom and settled myself for a long stay, despite the fact I still had an Airbnb rented in Los Angeles. I took a shower in the huge marble bathroom and sat on the ground while the numerous jets pummeled me with water, which felt like aqua therapy. I scrubbed every inch of my body and hair with the luxurious bath products provided and then wrapped myself in the exquisite robe and slippers.

After my scrub-down, I went into the living room and turned on the television. As luck would have it, Steve Jobs was there to show me a curated selection of news, travel, and adventures. I watched with fascination as I was shown all the incredible places around the world I would be going to. Steve indicated I would be saving many more people with my psychic healing powers all over the world. A trip to Scotland was up next for me, Steve let me know. He told me I needed to investigate my genealogy there. I was so excited about my future.

I fell asleep on the couch in front of the television and only woke up with the arrival of my next-door neighbors in the adjacent suite. They were loud and obviously drunk as they shouted and laughed and slammed the door as they entered. Once inside their suite, I couldn't hear them anymore.

I got up from the couch, turned off the television, and went to bed, this time in the bedroom. I got under the covers and marveled at the exceptional linens and fluffy down pillows. It felt like a dream come true, and I quickly fell back into the best sleep I'd had in ages. I left the drapes open to the Strip overnight and woke up to a beautiful sunrise.

Chapter 49
Exploring Las Vegas

I woke up after a solid twelve-hour sleep, devoid of dreams or interruptions. I was hungry again, realizing I had forgotten to eat dinner, so I decided to order breakfast before my appointment in the spa at ten o'clock. The room service menu was vast and offered many different types of cuisines.

I decided to order a South American breakfast of meat empanadas and a pot of coffee. While waiting for its delivery, I hopped in the shower, once again sitting on the marble floor, letting the water jets beat me from above. For some reason, this helped quiet my mind, and I felt I could stay in the shower for hours. I dressed quickly and picked my clothes for impact: four-inch, strappy black sandals, skinny black jeans, a white crochet top over a black cami, and enough bling to reflect the sun beating down on me.

The visit to the spa was lovely and a lot of fun. The beautiful, black spa manager did my treatments herself, and by the end of our time, I felt she had become a friend.

"Would you like to work with me one day?" I asked her as she moved from my fingers to my toes.

"Oh, Miss Liz, I could never do that to my boss," she replied as she looked up to the Trump logo above us. She looked back at me sincerely, and we both knew who she meant.

"Yeah, I couldn't do that to him either." I felt ashamed that I had even asked, as I instantly remembered the feeling I had when colleagues would steal my great employees from me back home in Seattle.

The bill for my manicure and pedicure was three times what I would have paid in Los Angeles, and I realized my stay in Trump Tower could end up costing me a lot if I continued to spend this way. While I had brought a lot of cash with me, I had the distinct desire to preserve it. I decided to lay low for the day and skip the cabana. I called the bell desk and asked to have my car pulled up.

I walked slowly in my heels and newly manicured toes on the shiny marble floor so as not to slip and fall. I held my head up high and tried to ignore the stares from the people around me. I grabbed a $20 bill out of my purse and handed it to the bellhop in exchange for my keys.

"Have a great day, Liz," he said as he shut the door.

"I will. Thanks!" I said as I drove away from the hotel.

I had no idea where I was going, so I turned on some music and headed for the Strip. A few moments later, the GPS came on spontaneously and asked if I would like the car to navigate the trip. I pressed the yes button and waited for my instructions.

The car did not disappoint, and soon I was traveling to Henderson, Nevada. I spent a few hours driving around the area and looking at homes from the street. I liked the desert climate and architecture; it felt comfortable and familiar. I stopped at a coffee shop and did more internet research on homes for sale. I had every intention of purchasing a home and took this opportunity to find where I wanted to live.

After touring Henderson, I decided to head back to the hotel. As I approached the entrance, I noticed the hotel was packed with cars and people milling about. I weaved around a few limos and parked my car near the bell desk. All the bellhops were busy, so I left the keys in the car and took a seat on a marble bench looking straight at the hotel entrance.

Throngs of people were all around me, talking excitedly and smoking cigarettes. I noticed that most everyone had foreign accents, and the couple next to me seemed to be from England.

"Hi. How are you today?" the elegantly dressed, middle-aged lady asked me in an impeccable English accent.

"I'm great! Are you from London?" I asked, hoping I was correct in my accent geography. Years earlier, I had mistakenly identified an Australian accent as British, which is usually a conversation non-starter.

"Yes!" she said excitedly. "Isn't this hotel incredible?"

"It sure is," I replied. "Say, may I have one of your cigarettes?"

"Of course," she said as she opened the top of the pack and motioned for me to take one.

"Wow, these are cool," I said as I pulled out one of the tiny, thin cigarettes.

"They're menthol, sorry," she said as she reached toward me and offered a lighter.

"I prefer menthol. Thank you so much," I said as I lit the cigarette.

I glanced at the cigarette box in her hand and asked if I could look closer at it, as it looked so different from the cigarette boxes in the United States. She handed it to me, and I was taken aback to see a picture of diseased, cancer-filled lungs on the front of the pack.

"This is how they try to deter us from smoking in the United Kingdom," she offered.

"Wow, that's pretty explicit," I replied.

The last time I had been to England, I hadn't been smoking cigarettes, so I had not seen this aversion therapy tactic before.

Chapter 50
David

I sat on the marble bench in front of the hotel and continued one of my favorite pastimes, watching people. Trump Tower Las Vegas was an incredible place to see and be seen. As I watched the crowds, I noticed a new figure at the bell stand, a very good-looking man, bronzed from the sun, wearing a chef's jacket and pants. I figured he must have come from the kitchen to hang out with the bellhops. I glanced back at him and noticed he was carrying a bunch of water bottles and was staring directly at me. I met his gaze and kept it as he walked toward me. He smiled at me and gave me a little wave as he approached.

"Hi. Would you like a bottle of water?" he asked as he held one out for me to take.

"Thank you!" I moved down on the bench a bit so he could sit next to me.

"What's your name?" he asked immediately as he held out his hand.

"Liz," I said. "What's yours?"

"David," he replied. "Nice to meet you."

I shook his hand and noticed they were filthy, like they hadn't been washed for weeks.

"Sorry about my dirty hands," he said, as I attributed the appearance of his hands to kitchen work. He was incredibly attractive and had bright-blue eyes that popped against his tanned skin and sun-bleached hair.

"When is your birthday?" I asked randomly on a psychic hunch and without any forethought.

"September ninth," he replied.

"No way," I said. "That is my birthday! Very cool."

We sat on the bench for a while and made small talk. I drank my water and wondered when David would have to go back to work in the kitchen, as I fancied his company.

"Are you working today?" I asked.

"No, I don't have a job," he replied.

I didn't expect that answer. "What's up with the chef's uniform?"

"I borrowed this from a friend," David replied.

"I see." I immediately wondered why, as it didn't seem to be a fashion trend to impersonate a chef.

I had run out of cigarettes and did not feel physically up to leaving the hotel again at that moment. I had glanced in the gift shop and hadn't seen any cigarettes, so I believed I would have to leave the premises to get them.

"How would you feel about running an errand for me in my car?" I impulsively asked David as I gestured to the G-Wag near the bell desk.

"Sure! What do you need?" he asked excitedly.

"I need cigarettes," I replied.

Smoking cigarettes was a relatively new activity for me, and I was very picky about what I would inhale. I truly believed from the messages on my television that one brand of cigarettes, and one brand only, could allow me to smoke without any harm, and I was obsessed with purchasing this hard-to-find brand. I knew that Las Vegas had smoke shops the size of Costco, so I hoped David could find one and bring the cigarettes back to me. Additionally, I thought it would be nice to see him again while I was in Las Vegas.

"Here," I said as I handed him an empty cigarette pack and stuffed two crisp $100 bills into it. "I'd like a carton, and you keep the change," I said. I had previously thought he had shoes on, but now I noticed he was barefoot. I handed David the keys to my new car and took a photo of him as he drove away.

"Be right back, Liz!" he shouted and waved out the window as he grinned from behind the wheel.

I turned around and noticed the British couple staring at me.

"Do you know that man?" the lady asked suspiciously with a puzzled look on her face.

"I do now!" I said as I walked back toward the hotel entrance but quickly realized that David and I hadn't exchanged phone numbers or any other way to identify each other. I decided to go up to my suite and wait for him and the cigarettes. I passed the guard at the elevators and flashed a big smile as I waved my room key and driver's license in front of him.

"Have a great day, Miss Liz," he said as I marveled at how all the staff seemed to know my name.

Once back in the suite, I fell sound asleep for several hours. I woke up just as the sun was setting, providing an eerie light over the Strip. I glanced at the clock and noticed it was now about seven at night. To be honest, I had completely forgotten about David, the car, and the cigarettes, and my mind was racing at an uncomfortable pace. I got up, went to the fridge, and poured myself a glass of leftover champagne. I sat on the sofa and stared out the window for a long time.

I was hungry: hungry for food, hungry for friendships, hungry for companionship, and hungry for answers to my unraveling life. I had to admit to myself that I felt alone and very vulnerable at that moment. I reached out to a few friends back home by text, but couldn't locate anyone. Illogically, I decided it was time to roam.

I changed into another outfit and headed toward the lobby in black platform sandals, black ripped jeans, a crisp, white linen shirt, and a black Alo hoodie I had purchased in the spa. I thought it looked great on me and felt like a model as I glided through the hotel to exit the entrance.

Before leaving, I stopped by the gift shop. "Where is the nearest place to buy a pack of cigarettes?" I asked the young man behind the counter.

"Right here," he replied as he gestured to the desk.

"But I don't see any cigarettes in here," I said.

"That's because we keep them back here," he replied as he opened the drawers behind the desk, displaying multiple brands.

"Do you carry this one?" I asked as I pulled an empty box from my purse.

"Yes, we sure do," he replied.

"I'll take two packs," I said as I handed him a crisp $100 bill.

"Ninety dollars is your change," he said as he counted and handed me the bills.

Only five dollars per pack? That's half the price of California! I said to myself.

Chapter 51
Family Ties

Elated at my cigarette purchase, I decided to sit outside and smoke one. I walked across the driveway under the porte cochere to the marble bench and took a seat. It was a surprisingly quiet night at the hotel, and few cars were in the front. I did not see my car and assumed that David had brought it back and the bellhop had put it away for the night. I did not think to ask anyone about it and continued my evening of people watching. As I now had cigarettes, it didn't seem urgent to find the spoils from David.

I noticed a very tall and extremely thin young man sitting on the bench next to mine. I looked at him in his sharp-looking suit, and he smiled back. After a couple of minutes, the man approached me and said, "Hi. I'm a realtor here. Are you looking for a condominium at Trump Tower by chance?"

I thought that sounded like an interesting idea, as I absolutely loved the property and thought I wanted to move to Las Vegas. "Maybe," I said. "How expensive are they?"

"They're not bad. I'm Scott, by the way," he replied as he held out his hand.

"Hi, Scott. I'm Liz," I said as I shook his hand. "I'm looking to move here, so perhaps we should talk."

"That would be great," he replied. "Here's my card. Call me anytime. I work 24/7. Got a wife and a kid to take care of," he finished.

I took his card and put it in my pants pocket for safekeeping. "I'll call you soon, Scott," I said as I opened the pack and pulled out a cigarette. "Would you like one?" I offered to him.

"Thank you. I would love one," he replied as he took the cigarette from my hand and proffered a lighter from his suit pocket to light both of our cigarettes.

We sat in silence and smoked our cigarettes as we watched the hustle and bustle of people arriving and departing from the hotel. After we were done with our cigarettes, Scott rose to his feet and stuck out his hand again. I shook it, and we promised to be in touch with each other very soon.

I watched Scott as he got into a beat-up old Honda and drove away. I wondered if real estate sales were lucrative for him and admired his drive to provide for his family. I promised myself I would call him soon to look at renting a condo at Trump Tower. I was very pleased at the way my stay in Las Vegas was going and started to relax a little bit.

I spent several days at Trump Tower, relaxing and working on my businesses from a perch in my beautiful suite. Occasionally, I would brave the heat and sit by the pool to get a little vitamin D, but mostly I stayed inside and low-key.

One evening, after a very productive day of computer work, I decided to go downstairs and have a cigarette on my favorite bench. I lit and smoked one cigarette after another that evening and began to pace around the front of the hotel. About an hour later, several cop cars came up to the front of the hotel and parked, but most of the police did not get out of their cars. I watched as they worked on their computers and spoke to each other over the CCB.

After about sixty minutes, the cops all drove away and left the hotel entrance deserted. I glanced nervously to my right and noticed a familiar Range Rover approaching, my son's. At first, I assumed my mind was playing tricks on me, but after verifying the license plate, I knew I had been found. I panicked and quickly hid behind a large bush at the entrance. But my son had spotted me already, and I knew there was no way out at that point.

My son parked in front of the hotel and approached me behind the bush. "Mom, what are you doing here? You gotta come back to Los Angeles with me."

I cowered from him against the wall of the hotel and said in the loudest voice I could muster, "Get away from me!"

"Mom! I'm here to help you!" he replied, sounding exasperated.

"You're here to kill me! How did you find me?" I screamed, wondering if the bellhops would hear me. I fully believed my son was there to harm me.

I began to get up from the ground, but found myself without a lot of power at that point. My emaciated limbs barely allowed me to get up, and when I did, I had to kick off the platform sandals to steady myself.

"You need to leave now, Michael," I said to my son. "If you don't, I'll call 911 and have you removed from the premises."

"Mom, don't be dumb. They won't remove me; they'll remove you," he said confidently.

I left my shoes on the ground and started to walk back into the hotel with a lit cigarette in my hand. I turned around and came back out to defiantly extinguish it in front of my son.

"Will you be here tomorrow, Mom?" he asked in a soft voice.

"Do not count on me being here tomorrow, Michael," I said, knowing full well that I would escape overnight now that I had been found.

I headed back toward my suite and exited the elevator on the penthouse floor, only to realize that I had left my phone on the marble bench downstairs. I decided to wait for a few minutes, hoping my son would go away. Once downstairs, I noticed the Range Rover was gone, so I thought the coast was clear.

I looked at the bench and noticed my phone was gone. I headed to the bell desk and asked, "Did anyone turn in a cell phone?"

"You mean this one, Liz?" a bellhop said as he held out my phone to me.

"Why yes, that's the one." I smiled, thanked him for the phone. I didn't have any cash on me to tip him, so I turned around to head back upstairs.

As I did, I ran directly into my son. He held out his arms and grabbed me by my bony shoulders, instantly immobilizing and overpowering me with his strength.

"Don't touch me!" I shouted in front of the bellhop as I shoved my son away from me.

My son was calm and said to me in a low, quiet voice, "Mom, I've called 911. You are going to the hospital."

Chapter 52
Unraveling in Las Vegas

I couldn't believe what I was hearing from my son. I suddenly felt like a caged animal, and all I could think about was escaping. With all the strength I could muster, I broke free from my son and bolted down the driveway away from the hotel. I ran fast, but my son ran faster.

He grabbed me from behind and swung me around to face him. "Mom! You are not okay!" he shouted at me as he held me again.

"I am perfectly fine, except for you!" I screamed back at him.

He continued to hold me tight against his body as I struggled to break free. I could hear an ambulance and a fire truck in the distance, and the closer they got, the more agitated I became.

"Mom, I'm not going to let you do this to yourself anymore," he said as the vehicles approached.

"Do what? I'm totally fine! What do you mean? Do what to myself?" I asked as I gave up the physical struggle.

Once the ambulance parked next to us in the driveway of the hotel, my son released his grasp on me. The medics got out of the ambulance, and the firefighters got out of the fire truck and formed a circle around us. Soon, my son and I were surrounded by those summoned to help me.

"This is my mom, Liz," Michael said to the EMS personnel. "She is in need of help."

"I don't need anything except for you to leave, Michael," I shouted back at anyone who would listen.

I could feel myself breaking with reality as I struggled to stay coherent. *How on Earth can I get myself out of this?* In a moment of lucidity, I recognized that if I had any hope of going back to my Trump Tower suite that night, I'd better calm down and be civil. My son was talking in a huddle with the ambulance drivers, so I decided to chat politely with the firefighters.

"I think you guys can go now," I said to the captain and tried to smile sweetly at him. "This is just a fight between my son and me. It's over now," I continued.

At that moment, one of the medics left my son and came over to speak with me. "Liz, your son has told us what's going on," he said to me.

"Oh good," I said. "I need to go back to my room now and get some sleep."

"I'd like to have a word with you privately, if I may, Liz," he replied as he gestured to the ambulance. "Please come have a chat with me over here."

I approached the ambulance with trepidation. Even though I had been raised in a medical household and had practiced medicine myself for twenty-plus years, I was suspicious of any attempt to help me at this point.

"Please step inside the rig," the medic said.

"I would prefer to talk out here," I said as I motioned to the pavement in front of me.

"We need to sit inside the ambulance and talk privately," he insisted.

Believing there were no other viable options that didn't involve digging myself even deeper in trouble, I reluctantly stepped up into the ambulance and took a seat on the gurney. The medic shut and locked the ambulance door behind me, and instantly I knew I was screwed.

Chapter 53

Hospitalized in Las Vegas

My son approached the rear door window at the back of the ambulance and waved us goodbye. The medic spoke to him through the closed window. "We are all set to go, Michael," the medic said. "I'm going to give your mom a Molotov cocktail now." My son gave him the thumbs-up sign in reply.

"There's no way in hell that you're giving me that!" I screamed.

I knew exactly what was in that syringe, and I knew exactly what it would do to me. It was a potent cocktail of three gnarly psychiatric drugs that would put me out for days. It would also cause me to lose control of my bladder.

"I will not allow you to give me that shot!" I screamed as loudly as I could.

My son looked on as the medic approached me with the syringe. I tried to swing my arms and hit the syringe out of his grasp to no avail.

The medic lunged at me and drove the needle into my deltoid. I screamed in pain as he pushed the devastating drugs into my system.

Within seconds, I went limp and could feel myself fade away as I lost control of my bladder. As I peed my pants, I hallucinated and thought I was in a warm bath. It was actually a very peaceful way to lose consciousness, as opposed to the nausea from being roofied. As I detached from reality, I could feel the four-point restraints being tightened around my body.

I woke up two days later in a hospital bed in Las Vegas. I had been placed on the medical floor because my chemistries were dangerously out of balance from my weight loss. Since admission, I had been pumped full of twenty liters of saline, among other things, and I did not like my new bloated physique. I vowed to get this water weight off me as soon as possible. I recovered as an inpatient for several more days and only had a Bible to read and Christian television stations to watch. I took the time to read Revelations, a chapter I had never read before. I found it to be fascinating but somewhat terrifying in my fragile state.

The days in the hospital passed slowly, and the nights were lonely and frightening. The very same environment that trained and employed me as a physician for nearly two decades—once bringing me peace and comfort—now terrified me with its austerity and detached visits from uninterested and overworked staff. While there, I did not hear from my son or anyone else in my life.

Finally, I was released on day seven of my stay. There was only one catch: the hospital had lost all my jewelry! My nurse attempted to discharge me several times, but I refused to leave as they asked me to sign a release stating I had received all my belongings prior to discharge.

Given that I had been wearing over $30,000 in jewelry at the time of admission, I escalated my complaint of missing jewels to the hospital administrator. Thankfully, she was able to locate the missing items a few hours later, and I was able to be discharged later that day. I tried to find out where my jewelry had been, clearly not in the hospital safe, but no one would give me any information.

I put back on the clothes I had been wearing when the ambulance picked me up, complete with pee stains, put all my jewelry back on, and walked out into the sunshine. I fortunately had my phone at that time, so I called an Uber to take me back to Trump Tower. Once there, I stopped by the bell desk to check on what had been happening while I was gone. I also realized I needed to find my car.

"Hello. I'm staying at the hotel, but I had to depart for a few days. I'm back now and wondering if you have my car."

"Do you have a ticket, ma'am?" the new bellhop asked.

"I don't actually," I replied. "I have a white Mercedes G-Wagon. It's been here for a while."

"Without a ticket, I can't help you," he said matter-of-factly.

At that moment, I couldn't remember what had happened to my car and why I didn't have a ticket. With all the trauma and drama of the past weeks, I had completely forgotten about David and the cigarette run.

Chapter 54

A Sad Goodbye

I walked inside the beautiful lobby of Trump Tower Las Vegas, not realizing it would be the last time I did so. I approached the front desk and asked for a new room key.

"May I please have a new key for suite 2208?" I asked as I handed her my driver's license.

"I'm sorry, ma'am. You have been moved out of the hotel," she answered.

"Moved out?" I asked in disbelief.

What the hell? This can't be happening! My mind raced, and my heart began to quicken.

"Yes, after the incident the other night, management decided it would be best if you no longer stayed with us. The hotel packed up your things, and they are waiting for you at the bell stand," she finished as she handed me a bell ticket.

I couldn't believe what I was hearing. I was devastated and embarrassed, and I wasn't sure what to do at that point, without my car.

"Thank you," I said sheepishly as I turned around to exit the hotel and started to tear up. "Oh, I need to get into the vault." I remembered my money and turned back around to face the receptionist.

"Certainly, ma'am," she said as she gestured to follow her to the vault.

I walked past the expressionless armed guard as I wiped tears from my cheeks. I quickly gathered my satchel of cash and exited the lobby. I approached the bell desk again and tipped them generously as they brought out my huge suitcase and bag after bag of items they had gathered from my suite in their eponymous laundry bags. I scoured my mind for what I could possibly do now. I had no car, no hotel room, and a whole lot of stuff to lug around in the heat.

Fortunately, I had the presence of mind to remember my new friend, Scott. I moved all my belongings from the bell stand to my favorite smoking bench under the porte cochere and pulled out Scott's card.

He answered cheerily on the first ring. "Hello, Scott here. How may I help you?"

"Hi, Scott. This is Liz. We met a few days ago at Trump Tower," I replied.

"Hi, Liz!" he answered. "How are you?"

"Well, not so great at the moment," I answered. "I'm at Trump Tower but need another place to stay. Can you help me with that?"

"I'm right around the corner, Liz, showing an apartment to another client. Can I pick you up in fifteen minutes?" he asked.

"That would be wonderful," I replied, feeling like a piece of shit.

Although I had been kicked out of Trump Tower, they still let me sit outside on the property and smoke with the other guests. I chain-smoked until Scott pulled up in his beater car.

"Hi, Liz! Hop in!" he said through an open passenger window as he stopped next to me. He got out to help me with all my luggage and struggled to fit it into the small car. "Wow, you don't pack light, do you?"

"Sorry, I left Los Angeles in a hurry and packed too much stuff," I replied.

"No problem. You will have your own room at my house, so it will fit just fine."

Chapter 55

Scott

I hadn't realized that I would be staying with Scott and his family, but was in no shape to protest or ask for different accommodations. It seemed kind of sweet. Here I was in a big, new city with a stranger, and he was inviting me to stay in his home with his family.

I'm looking forward to meeting your family," I said as Scott pulled out of Trump Tower and headed for the strip, weaving his way through the afternoon traffic. "Where do you live, Scott?"

"I live in a little neighborhood northeast of Las Vegas," he replied.

I took in the sights around me as we drove in dense traffic for over thirty minutes. The Strip was long gone, and now we drove our way into seedier and seedier neighborhoods. Metal bars on the windows and doors were the norm, and I began to see numerous homeless people walking on the sidewalks with shopping carts carrying their possessions.

"Are you a Las Vegas native?" I asked as we continued to his home.

"Oh, Liz, I've got a story for you," he replied.

"Don't we all, Scott," I said, thinking of my life's drama of late.

He then continued to tell me that he was an only child and a recent transplant to Las Vegas from Cuba. Both of his parents had been tortured and killed by Castro, leaving him an orphan at a young age. His grandmother had raised him until he was old enough to immigrate to the United States by himself.

"Holy crap, Scott. That's terrible. I'm so sorry," I said as I felt self-conscious about my inquiry in the first place.

Scott finally turned off the main drag and into a small neighborhood. The houses were tiny and dilapidated, most with chain-link fences housing menacing-looking dogs barking on metal leashes. Scott got out of the car and unlocked the chain-link fence protecting his driveway and family.

We emptied all my stuff from his car and walked to the front door. The tiny front yard was littered with garbage, toys, overgrown grass, and near-dead plants in desperate need of water. I noticed a broken screen on the front door and a stained dish towel used as a curtain in the kitchen window. We entered the home, and I immediately heard a screech coming from another part of the house.

"Scott, is that you?" a female voice asked in a sharp tone. "Are you *finally* here?"

"Yes, sweetheart, I'm home. I have a guest with me," Scott answered.

Scott motioned for me to continue to follow him through the tiny house. I dragged my suitcase behind me and noticed the contents of the house were completely trashed. It made a garage sale look like designer décor in comparison. Laundry, not sure if it was clean or dirty, sat piled in every corner of each room.

We walked past the tiny kitchen with a hot plate and mini fridge, and I noticed empty to-go containers and dirty dishes everywhere.

"Sorry about the mess," Scott said to me. "My wife isn't very good at housework."

I couldn't believe they lived in this squalor and wondered if the place was even remotely sanitary. *Well, this is a big change from Trump Tower*, I thought to myself, but was grateful for the place to stay.

"Here, put your stuff in this bedroom," Scott said as we entered what was clearly his young son's room. The tiny bedroom had a miniature bed and enough stuffed animals to fill Disneyland.

"Scott Jr. will sleep with us while you are here," he announced.

"I can totally sleep on the couch, Scott, so your son can have his own bed," I stated.

"We don't have a couch yet, Liz. The real estate market has been a little rough lately."

Chapter 56
Deborah

I put my things down in Scott Jr.'s room and followed Scott into his bedroom, where his wife was propped up with pillows watching a movie and texting her friends while her child played on another iPhone.

"Scott! Where is my food?" she screamed at him.

"I'm sorry, sweetie, but I haven't had a chance to pick it up yet," he replied.

"You are such a fucking loser," she screamed. "Go get it now!"

Scott hadn't even had a chance to introduce me before he turned on his heels and guided me out of the bedroom. "Let's go. Come with me," he said as he headed out the front door.

I truly couldn't imagine staying in the house without him, so I gladly followed him back to the car. "What are you getting for your wife?" I asked as we drove a short distance.

"I always get all of her favorite foods, every day, on my way home from work," he answered.

We pulled into a rundown strip mall not far from his house, and I noticed the garbage on the ground, complete with syringes, needles, and condoms.

"Wait here," he said as he left the car running and entered a convenience store. I wondered if this was just a quick detour before we got to a restaurant. I didn't have to wait long for an answer as Scott came out of the store quickly with his arms full of food: a large watermelon slushy, a huge Diet Coke, a giant Snickers bar, Funyuns, jalapeño poppers, and a bag of double-stuffed Oreos. I marveled at the haul and wondered where that tiny woman (girl, really) was going to put all this junk food.

"Deborah is very particular about the food she eats," he said as he got into the car.

"What do you mean, *particular?*" I asked, thinking that most people who were particular about food in the Pacific Northwest wouldn't touch the stuff he had just purchased.

"Well, she's very particular about the junk food she eats," he elaborated. "I've tried to get her to eat other stuff, but she refuses."

I wondered what the little boy ate. *Hopefully something healthier than that,* I thought.

We drove the quick drive back to his house in silence. I was starting to feel uncomfortable with his living arrangement and his wife. She didn't seem very nice or appreciative of Scott's efforts.

We got out of the car, and I helped him carry the spoils to Deborah. Once in the bedroom at the foot of the bed, she screamed at

Scott and instructed him to bring the food to her bedside. Scott complied and placed the items next to her.

"Where the fuck are my Doritos?" she asked incredulously.

"I'm sorry, Deborah. I forgot them," he replied while looking down at his feet.

"You are such an asshole! Go back and get my Doritos *now!*" she screeched.

I looked at Scott and noticed he looked completely defeated. "Okay, my darling, I will go back and get the Doritos."

Chapter 57

Foraging for Food

By this time, it was past 8:00 p.m., and I wondered what we were going to do for dinner. We drove back to the convenience store, again in silence. When Scott returned to the car with a large bag of Cool Ranch Doritos, I asked him if she always treated him that way.

"Not all the time," he answered. "Sometimes she is nice to me."

I realized the junk food he had purchased was the only food he had purchased, and I wondered what food he and his son would eat for dinner.

"What are you doing for dinner?" I asked as we drove back.

"Scott Jr. and I will find something in the house. I'll fix something for you, too, Liz," he added.

I felt it would potentially be insulting if I offered to buy dinner for the family so soon, so I kept my mouth shut.

"Don't worry about me. I've got some weight to get off me," I added, referring to the hospital water weight.

"Liz, you are tiny," he replied.

I intellectually knew he was right, but my body dysmorphia took hold, so I elected not to reply to his statement of fact.

We entered the house again, and I found myself with a sense of dread. I did not like his wife so far and didn't feel comfortable in their home. *Perhaps this isn't such a good idea after all,* I thought to myself. *What are my options at this point?*

I decided not to follow Scott back into the bedroom where his wife was. I could hear every word, though, as she continued to berate him for his shortcomings in purchasing the junk food. I truly wondered why he put up with it. He seemed like such a kind and sincere young man.

Scott came out of the bedroom and asked me to join him in the kitchen with his son. He carried Scott Jr. in his arms and placed him in a highchair at the table. I figured he must be about three, so I asked him, "How old are you, three?"

"I'm six!" he shouted while waving four fingers at me.

I knew enough pediatrics to know this was a problem, and it had an official name, *failure to thrive,* consistent with the little boy's environment.

"Scott, may I help you make some dinner?" I asked.

"Nope, we're all set. Nothing fancy, but it is food," he continued as he brought three steaming bowls of chicken-flavored ramen and three pieces of bare white toast to the table.

"I'm sorry, but we don't have anything but water to drink," he said as he sat down and put a glass of rust-colored liquid in front of me.

"It's all good," I said as I dove into the ramen. "I forgot how dang good this stuff is." I twirled the noodles on my plastic fork. The white bread, dipped in the ramen broth, was likewise just as good, and I appreciatively ate everything he gave me.

After dinner, I retired to Scott Jr.'s room and tried to fall asleep on the tiny bed without a pillow. I tried my level best to be grateful for the shelter, but I felt edgy and uncomfortable. Finally, and well past midnight, I fell into a fitful sleep.

The next morning, I woke to the sound of a rooster. *Where is there a rooster in this hood?* I wondered. It seemed more than a little out of place given the poor, urban area I found myself in. I could also hear a dog barking loudly, and the sound seemed to be coming from the backyard.

I stepped through the tiny kitchen to the only other door in the house that led outside. The door had broken glass and a missing deadbolt. I opened it and found myself staring at a big, intimidating dog in the chained-in neighbor's yard, only a few feet from where I was standing. I looked to my left and saw a very old, rusting washer and dryer hooked up outside the house. To my right, I saw a carport and a small patch of dirt with toys strewn about the ground.

The dog barked ferociously at me as I walked to the carport, stepping over McDonald's Happy Meal toys, broken bikes and trikes, and endless junk food containers and wrappers. As I headed to the carport, a large rat ran by my feet and disappeared under the house. It took all my might not to scream and run away.

As I approached the carport hanging off the side of the tiny house, I could hear Deborah talking with Scott Jr. She was using a sweet, high-pitched tone with him, and I was glad to see she didn't treat her son like she treated her husband.

"Good morning, Deborah. Hi, Scottie," I said as I rounded the corner.

"Scottie, say good morning to Liz," she said as she ignored me and spoke through her son. He immediately got shy and turned his head away from me.

"Does Scottie go to school yet?" I asked innocently.

"No, we are homeschooling him," she replied.

I wondered what that really meant, given the circumstances.

"Oh, that's interesting," I said as I took a seat in the carport in a miniature chair, clearly meant for Scottie. "I don't want to be in your hair today, Deborah," I said as I lit a cigarette. Honestly, what I meant was that I didn't want her in *my* hair.

"Don't worry about that. Scott said he would come back on his lunch hour to pick you up. Can I bum a cigarette from you?" Deborah asked.

I handed her a half-filled pack of cigarettes and a lighter. After she had lit one, Scottie excitedly said, "Mommy! You have fire in your mouth!"

I glanced at my watch and realized that Scott's lunch hour wasn't too far away, so I decided to get cleaned up. "I'm going to go take a shower," I said as I got up and went back into the house, leaving my cigarettes and lighter with her.

I showered quickly in my flip-flops as the bathroom looked like it hadn't been cleaned in years. I dressed in all white to prepare for the heat: white jeans, white cami, white baseball cap, white leather tennis shoes, and a white denim jacket. Even the diamonds I wore that day were colorless.

I exited the house and went back to the carport. Deborah and Scottie were gone, so I sat on the single adult chair and lit another cigarette. I was desperate for a cup of coffee, but knew it was a lost cause in that home. I felt intense shame at being kicked out of Trump Tower and contemplated returning to Los Angeles.

Chapter 58
The Car

After a few minutes, Scott drove up and hopped out of his vehicle. "Hey, Liz!" he shouted at me.

"Hi, Scott! Can I hang out with you this afternoon?" I asked.

"Yes, that's why I'm here. Let's go!" he said as he helped me up from the chair. "I'm going to show you some places you might want to rent in this town."

"That's awesome, Scott, but I also need to find my car," I replied as Scott opened my door for me.

"I didn't know you had a car, Liz," he replied.

"I do, but I don't know where it is," I said softly. "I think I might have given it away to a guy at Trump Tower," I continued, hardly believing what I was saying myself.

"We'll find it. Don't you worry," he said as he started the car and drove away from the house.

We drove back toward the Strip and carried on a casual conversation.

"Where are we going?" I asked as we inched our way in traffic.

"To the police precinct," he replied.

I was simultaneously grateful and terrified, as I had come to distrust most everyone in a position of authority. We pulled into the station and parked.

"Scott, I am pretty worried about this visit to the police," I said.

"Don't worry, Liz. Everything will be okay. I'm here for you," he said as he opened my door. I reluctantly got out of the car and walked with him into the building.

"Hello. We are here to locate my friend's car," Scott said to the stern-looking woman behind the desk.

"What happened to your car?" she asked me, expressionless.

"I gave it to a friend to run an errand, and he never came back," I replied, ashamed of the truth in front of Scott.

"How long ago?" she asked.

I searched my shaky memory for any details I could remember. "I think it was a week or two ago."

"Go ahead and have a seat. I'll have one of our officers come speak with you," she finished.

We sat down on two very worn chairs and waited. After about fifteen minutes, an officer approached us and said, "Come with me."

We followed him dutifully to a small interrogation room and sat down across from him at a table.

"I heard why you are here," he said, looking directly at me. "Please tell me your story in your own words."

I told him everything I could remember about that day at Trump Tower, which wasn't much. He listened intently and then excused himself for a few minutes. When he returned, he tossed a few papers at me across the table.

"Is this your car?" he asked.

I glanced at the pictures before me and said, "Yes, that's my Mercedes."

"Your car was left at the Cigarette Emporium by a man who was arrested in the store. He was picked up because the store clerk was suspicious of why a barefoot guy in a chef's uniform was driving this new $150,000 car without a license or ID. He also had two $100 bills and tried to purchase a carton of cigarettes."

Oh, good Lord, I thought. *Had I caused David to be arrested? How would I ever reach him again to apologize?*

"Do you know what happened to him?" I asked.

"He told us that he lived on the streets near the Strip. That's probably where he is right now, but I don't recommend looking for him. What's a nice girl like you doing with a homeless guy like him anyway?" the cop asked.

"It's a long story." I was not in the mood to go deeper on this topic in front of Scott. I was humiliated enough as it was without airing any more of my dirty laundry to him.

"How can I get my car?" I asked the cop.

"It's been impounded," he replied.

"What does that mean?" I asked reflexively.

"It means it will cost you a lot of money to get it out," he replied.

"Where is my car?" I continued.

"It's at County Line," he replied.

"That's about fifty miles away," I stated, having passed it on my drive into Las Vegas from Los Angeles.

"Yes, it is," he confirmed.

"Who do I pay to get the car out of hawk?" I asked.

"You pay them," he replied. "Just so you know, we did try to reach you on Facebook when we learned that you are the owner of the car."

"Facebook?" I replied in disbelief that this was the way the police would try to locate me. "I haven't used Facebook in years, which is why you didn't find me there." I shook my head.

When did Facebook become the first or preferred mode of communication for law enforcement? I wondered as the cop handed me the paperwork I would need to get my car released.

It wasn't possible for Scott to take me to County Line, so I parted ways with him at the precinct and ordered an Uber. The ride was long and very hot. If the car had air-conditioning, it certainly didn't work well at all. I arrived at County Line in a puddle of sweat.

We pulled into the address I was given, and I noticed it was a junkyard. I entered the single-wide trailer that appeared to be the office and looked for a human. No one was there. I decided to brave the heat and go outside to see if I could find my car.

Chapter 59

County Line

The scenery at County Line was something right out of an old Western, complete with tumbleweeds and the wavy lines of hot energy elevating from the ground. And the heat was fierce. I looked in the distance and thought I saw my car. But before I could walk there, a man appeared out of nowhere and said, "Can I help you, miss?"

"Hi, yes. I need to get my car," I said as I gestured toward where I thought it was.

"You have the white G-Wagon?" he asked. "We didn't know if you would ever come and get it. It's not every day that we see a car like that out here, especially if it's in good condition."

"It's been a rough couple of weeks. Can we please get my car?" I asked impatiently, anxious to get out of the heat.

"You gotta settle up before we do that," he replied.

I followed him back to the trailer office and braced myself for the total.

"That comes to $3,000," the man said as he handed me some papers to sign.

Ouch, I thought to myself as I handed him my metal Platinum AmEx card in return.

"You don't see these cards very often out here either!" he said as he began to write out my card number on an old credit card slip. "You must be rich!" he said as he gleefully completed the transaction.

"Not rich," I said, "just fortunate, I guess."

"Well, I'd like to be fortunate like you, miss," he said as he led me out of the office back into the heat.

If he only knew what a disaster my life has become, I thought to myself.

We had to walk a great distance to the car, past innumerable junkers, old fridges, tractors no longer working, and other appliances.

"Where are the keys?" I asked.

"They are in the car," he replied.

That seems a little unsafe, I thought as we approached the vehicle. I investigated the car through the driver's side window and let out a little groan. I had brought a lot of dark chocolate with me when I came to Las Vegas for one of my work projects, and it had stayed in the car throughout my time there. Nevada heat and chocolate do not go well together, and I saw I had a large puddle of chocolate on the passenger seat that was dripping onto the floor below.

I opened the door and took a seat behind the wheel. The car smelled like chocolate, but it did not smell good to me. I checked the gas gauge and saw I had little gas to make the fifty-mile trip back to Las Vegas.

"Sir, where is the closest gas station?" I asked through my open window.

"We've got gas right here, miss. I'll meet you over by the office where the pump is," he said as he turned around and started walking back.

I pulled up to the single pump and searched for a price per gallon. No such sign existed, so I placed the gas pump into my tank and started to fill it. After a very long time, the pump clicked to tell me it was done, twenty gallons, but still no price.

"How much do I owe you?" I asked.

"One hundred and eighty dollars," he replied, "but we only take cash for gas."

The gas was $9 per gallon, and normal gas prices at that time were around two dollars per gallon at a proper gas station. I realized at that point I had left my satchel of cash at Deborah and Scott's house, and I hoped that wouldn't be a problem. I scraped together $180 from the cash in my purse and thanked the man.

"Hope to see you again, miss," he shouted as I drove away.

Little did I know what a prophetic statement that would turn out to be.

Chapter 60
Back to Las Vegas

The drive back to Las Vegas was uneventful but long and hot. As I approached the Strip, I called Scott to get his address. We decided to meet at his house and plan the evening. I parked in his neighborhood and waited for Scott to arrive, as I really didn't want to have to deal with Deborah alone. Once there, he unlocked the chain-link gate and let me into the driveway and parked next to me.

"Wow, nice car!" Scott said to me as he walked around the perimeter.

"Thanks. It's my dream car," I replied, but as soon as I said it, I thought maybe I should start calling it my nightmare car, as it hadn't seemed to live up to its dream status.

Let's blame the car, Liz. That makes perfect sense.

"Hey, Scott," I said, "I'd really like to buy you guys dinner tonight."

"Liz, that is not necessary."

"But you've done a lot for me, and I am truly grateful. Please pick a restaurant and place an order. I'll give you my credit card," I replied.

"That would be nice, Liz. How about Thai?" he asked.

"Whatever you want, Scott. I'm chill with anything."

I stepped inside the house and immediately heard Deborah screaming at Scottie. *What on Earth could that little boy have done to deserve her wrath?* I wondered.

I was getting more and more uncomfortable in the house by the hour, so I immediately went to Scottie's room and shut the door. I sat on the bed and cupped my face in my hands. *What the fuck am I doing here?* I asked myself. *Maybe I should go back to Los Angeles tonight,* I thought.

As I rested on the side of the bed, my phone vibrated with a new text message. I looked over to see it was from Michael, my estranged son. I hadn't spoken with him since I was drugged and taken away from Trump Tower. My stomach churned with fear as I opened the text. It read:

I know you are still in Vegas. Meet me tomorrow for lunch at Wynn. Terrace Pointe Café at noon.

That's all it said. *Is he here, too?* I wondered. *Is he coming all the way over here from Los Angeles to have lunch with me?* I was confused, scared, and starting to feel again like I was losing touch with reality.

I laid down on the bed and closed my eyes. The cacophony of sights, sounds, jumbled reasoning, and overwhelming noise in my head made me feel like it would explode. I curled up into a fetal position on the small bed and buried my head into a large stuffed animal, trying to shut out the light in the room. I fell asleep for an undetermined amount of time and woke up to a knock at the door.

"Liz, I need your credit card," Scott said through the door.

"Sorry! Here it is," I said as I opened the door and handed him my AmEx.

"Thanks. Dinner should be here soon." He began to read my credit card number into the phone.

I decided I shouldn't be so antisocial, so I put on shorts, a T-shirt, and flip-flops and left the bedroom to find everyone else. I found them, all three, sitting in the carport, eating junk food. Scott had clearly gone on his requisite run while I was asleep. They didn't have a fourth chair, so I joined them and sat on the ground. I prayed that the rat wouldn't come back as I took my seat on the dusty, filthy ground.

A few minutes later, a car pulled up, and Scott got up to get the food delivery. He brought several bags back to us and began to take the food out of the bags. Scott handed me the receipt, and I scanned it quickly, but long enough to see the total, $210. *Wow!* I thought. *That is more than the suite at Trump!*

Deborah looked disinterested in the food, but Scott and Scottie dug in like they hadn't eaten in a week. I took a little for myself but left the vast majority for the boys.

"My son wants to have lunch with me tomorrow at Wynn," I blurted out.

"You have a son?" Scott asked in disbelief. I guess it hadn't come up in conversation yet.

"Actually, I have two sons," I replied. "Twenty-two and twenty-five."

"Holy crap, Liz. I honestly thought you were around twenty-five yourself," Scott confessed.

"That's very nice of you to say, Scott," I replied, both flattered and embarrassed at his compliment.

The boys finished the food and declared they were going to watch television together. I cleaned up the food boxes while Deborah spent time on her phone. I put the trash in the overflowing can near the chain-link fence and headed back into the house. It was clear that Scott and Scottie were watching monster trucks, and I felt my frazzled brain couldn't take the noise of the show, so I went back to bed.

I tried to drown out the noise of the television in the adjacent bedroom by listening to my favorite music, but even that was adding to my distress and restlessness. My mind was like a cement mixer, constantly churning with thick, heavy, dense thoughts. Finally, in a fit of desperation, I put a large stuffed animal over my head and eventually fell asleep.

Chapter 61
Lunch at Wynn

I woke up the next morning to the sound of the rooster. As I opened my eyes, I remembered that I was going to see my son that day, and an immediate sense of dread came over me. Our last touchpoint at Trump Tower was anything but good. I was kind of angry that no one from my family had been in touch with me over the previous weeks, including a hospitalization, and it added to the deep pain I was carrying around since childhood. I knew I could have been a better daughter, wife, and mother over the years, but I didn't expect them to abandon me during my time of need.

I took a shower and dressed casually, in white jeans, white tennis shoes, and a soft-pink sleeveless shirt. I paced outside under the carport for a couple of hours, smoking one cigarette after another until it was time to leave for Wynn. Scott had gone to work before I got up, and it really didn't seem necessary to say goodbye to Deborah. I let myself out of the chained-in parking space and headed to the Strip.

I pulled into Wynn and left my car with the bellhop. My stomach was in knots as I approached the outdoor restaurant, and I gave several thoughts to turning around and bailing on my son.

"Table for one?" the hostess asked.

"Actually, I'm meeting my son here, Michael. Do you know if he's here yet?" I asked.

"Oh, yes. They are here," she replied.

"Did you say they?" I asked.

"Your son is here with a woman," she replied.

Who the hell is here with Michael? I was in no mood to see anyone else and thought again about turning around and leaving.

As I followed the hostess to the table, I saw that my son had brought his girlfriend from Los Angeles with him. As I approached the table overlooking the pool, my son stood to greet me, still chivalrous despite our fractured relationship.

"Hi, Michael," I said as I faced him.

"Mom," he said as he gestured to sit in the chair in front of me. I glanced at his girlfriend briefly and said, "Hello."

I think she said "Hi" back, but I'm honestly not sure. She looked about as happy as I was to be there. I sat down at the table, and my son and I immediately got into it.

"Mom, you need help," my son said to me.

"Thank you, Michael, but I really don't need your help at this point. I'm fine. I am moving to Las Vegas."

"Mom, you're anything but fine," he shot back.

The waiter brought us coffee and took our order. I looked around me at the restaurant and noticed all the happy-seeming, wealthy-looking, beautiful people, and all I could see was what a loser I had become. I didn't feel I belonged at the likes of Wynn or Trump Tower anymore, and all I could think about was my escape from my son.

"Why are we here, Michael?" I asked wearily.

"Mom, you're coming back to Los Angeles with us after lunch," Michael replied.

Our lunches arrived, and I looked at the massive chicken and waffle spread before me. Although it smelled amazing and I was terribly hungry, I felt nauseated and was in no mood to eat.

Before my son could stop me, I leaped to my feet and scurried through the restaurant back inside the hotel. I glanced back at the table and saw Michael's girlfriend following me. I darted from left to right as I weaved through throngs of people and into the massive, red-carpeted hallway. I ran as fast as I could, ignoring the shouts from behind.

"Liz! Stop! Come back!" I heard her shout as I sped away on foot. Even though Michael's girlfriend wasn't even half my age, I handily outran her due to my newfound physique and strength.

I felt invincible as I ran farther and faster than I ever had before. After a while, I slowed down and noticed I was no longer being chased. I power-walked through the casino and exited the hotel. I handed my ticket to the man at the bell stand and waited nervously for my car, constantly checking to see if I had been followed.

My thirty minutes of parking cost $30. As I did not want to wait for change, I handed the bellhop a crisp $100 bill, grabbed my keys out of his hand, and quickly hopped behind the wheel.

"Mom!" I heard my son shout as I pulled out from Wynn onto Las Vegas Boulevard.

I rolled down the window and waved goodbye as I sped away. I had no idea where I was going to go, but I knew I had to get away from my son. I didn't have the presence of mind to think about the fact that most of my worldly possessions and cash were at Scott and Deborah's home, so I decided the best course of action was to head back to Los Angeles.

Chapter 62

From Bad to Worse

I drove down the Strip and got on to the 15 heading back to Los Angeles. I was shaking with adrenaline as I realized how tired and hungry I was. I reached over to the passenger seat and grabbed a few pieces of chocolate that were now solid after melting at the junkyard and shoved them into my mouth.

After a few miles on the highway, I realized I had no gas. I remembered the closed gas station I found on my way to Las Vegas, and I panicked. I was convinced I would never find fuel, so I pulled off the next exit and began to cry. I felt like my whole world was crashing down on me, and I truly didn't know what to do.

My only anchor, my earnest and eldest son, had become my enemy in my mind, and going back to Los Angeles only meant I would once again be in the same city as him. Nothing seemed like a good option as tears flowed down my face and I began to hyperventilate.

In my confused and near-delirious state, I looked up and saw the red emergency call button in my car. I pressed the button and waited.

"Mercedes-Benz emergency services," a pleasant voice said to me through the sound system.

"Hi. I need help," I said to the car in a soft voice.

"How can I help you?" the nice lady asked.

"I need gas, and there are no open gas stations. I also think I am going to die," I blurted.

There was a long pause of silence. Then she said, "You need gas, and you think you're going to *die?*"

"Yes, I think I am dying," I finished.

I don't remember much after that. The kind lady at Mercedes asked me my name and told me to "stay with her." I rested my head back on the headrest and lost consciousness while listening to the sound of approaching sirens.

My next recollection was waking up in the same hospital I had just been discharged from. Only this time, I wasn't on the medical floor. I had earned a bed in the psychiatric ward of a seedy Las Vegas hospital.

Chapter 63
Las Vegas Psychiatric Ward

I came to in a sterile, austere room typical of a psych ward. I knew them well, albeit from the other side. During my residency, I had worked for several years admitting patients to the psych ward to make extra income for my family and supplement my minimum-wage salary.

I lifted my head off the rubber-clad pillow and saw it was still daylight. I got out of bed and realized I was locked in the room. I went into the mirrorless bathroom and sat on the cold metal, seatless toilet rim. Being a patient in a psych ward was humiliating enough, but there were lots of other degrading aspects of being an inpatient in the loony bin: shoes without laces; meals without forks or knives; no personal care items; no combs or brushes; and my favorite, lukewarm coffee. (A prior resident had thrown hot coffee on another, necessitating the removal of all hot liquids.)

Being an inpatient in a psychiatric ward is as low as you can go, except for jail, which I had also experienced in my recent past. In both institutions, there is a pecking order and hierarchy to be followed, if not respected. Both share the highly sought-after activity of cigarette smoking, and mealtimes are simultaneously welcomed and dreaded: welcomed because you might get to get out of the ward or your cell; and dreaded because of the heightened danger of unstable inmates mulling about. Keeping your head down and avoiding eye contact are essential to surviving both.

An orderly came to my door and unlocked it. He entered and said, "It's time for dinner, Liz."

He handed me a pair of oversized orange scrubs and said, "I'll wait for you in the hall. Everyone else is already in the dining room."

I laughed as I put on the huge scrubs and whispered to myself, "I guess orange *really is* the new black." I exited my room.

The orderly unlocked door after door, and we walked for a long time down several corridors to reach the cafeteria. He unlocked and held open the final door, and I walked into a huge room that looked like a school gym. Rows and rows of tables were housing a mess of food and humans, and the dissonance of noise rattled my fragile psyche.

The orderly walked me to the food area and motioned for me to get a tray. I instead decided to get a cup of tepid coffee first, but the lady serving behind the counter screamed at me, "Stop! You must get food first!" Her shrill command scared me so badly that I spilled the cup of coffee. "See what you did!" she continued. "You idiots in here can't follow directions."

I turned back to my tray and looked at the options before me, "Chicken or beef?" she asked impatiently in an irritated tone as she held a large spoon over what looked like inedible slop.

"I'll just have the salad," I replied.

"You can't get no salad if you don't take a meat," she said loudly while rolling her eyes.

I was beginning to realize this visit to the hospital would be all about rules and rule-following. My survival depended on learning and adhering to those rules as fast as I could.

I learned the next day that I had been placed on a legal hold, a "5150," so I couldn't just leave when I felt better. I would have to go before a panel of judges to be discharged, and those hearings were set for over a week away.

My time in the loony slammer passed very, very slowly, and my days were marked by inedible meals and cigarette breaks. Ironically, the hospital provided the cigarettes, although not the "safe" kind I liked to smoke, and this provided us with four outdoor breaks per day, which was everything to us. The pecking order continued in the smoking area, and I did my level best to just stay to myself to avoid any conflict.

The residents of the psych ward varied from alcohol and drug addicts—actively detoxing from their substances—to others of us with different mental health diagnoses. Most of us were quite unstable, at least at the beginning of our stay, and it made for a miserable experience with little to no therapeutic benefit. Two men on the ward, including a vet in a wheelchair, were obsessed with my arms. Both tried to touch me and followed me around 24/7, even though this was strictly forbidden on the ward. The nurses were great in running interference for me, but it was very unsettling, and I didn't feel physically or emotionally safe during my stay.

The ancillary care team was generally compassionate and occasionally pleasant, but the physicians were honestly the worst I have ever worked with on either side of the fence. The physicians in this Las Vegas psychiatric ward were an absolute impediment to any healing that could have taken place and delivered substandard care to their patients. It was a truly life-changing, miserable experience I wouldn't wish on my worst enemy. Something must change in our mental health medical system.

The day of the hearing finally arrived, and I sat in a bare room all alone and participated in a video proceeding. The judges asked me a lot of questions about the events leading up to the hospitalization. I must have done well because before I could figure out what was going on, one of the judges slammed down a gavel and declared me free. I stood up from the table and said, "Thank you, Your Honors."

As if on cue, the orderly immediately opened the locked door behind me and said, "Congrats, Liz. You're getting out."

We walked back to my room, and housekeeping had already been called to turn over my room, getting prepared for the next unlucky resident. I quickly gathered my few belongings—just the clothes on my back—and was led to security to pick up my purse, phone, jewelry, and ID. I apparently wasn't wearing shoes in the car, so I likewise didn't have shoes at time of discharge. No effort was made whatsoever by the hospital to ensure I would be safe, have a ride, or be appropriately dressed upon discharge.

An orderly took me to a side entrance of the hospital and quickly waved me goodbye as he shut and locked the door behind him. I turned around to see a parking lot without any shade or place to sit, and the asphalt was scorching. I pulled out my phone from my purse and stared at it for a long time. It finally hit me after about ten minutes in the beating sun that I was still in Las Vegas and my stuff was at Scott's house. I called him and was relieved when he answered right away.

"Liz!" he shouted into the phone. "Are you okay? Where have you been? Where are you now?" He kept the rapid-fire questions coming without giving me a chance to answer.

"Scott!" I finally interrupted. "I'm at a hospital and need to be picked up."

"No problem, Liz. I'm on my way," he replied. "Share your location with me, and I'll pick you up."

Chapter 64
The Car, Again

About ten minutes later, Scott pulled up and shoved open the front passenger door before he came to a full stop.

"Are you okay, Liz?" he asked me right away after I got in.

"Not really," I replied. "I need to go to a pharmacy."

"Sure, no problem," he replied.

We drove in silence for a while before turning into a Walgreens parking lot.

Scott parked the car and turned to me and said, "Liz, what happened to you? You were supposed to come back and stay with us. I haven't heard from you in over a week!"

"I know, Scott. I'm so sorry. I had to go back to the hospital again." I didn't have the courage to tell him what was going on with me. The shame, guilt, and humiliation washed over me like an ocean wave, and I started to tear up.

"Liz, how can I help?" Scott asked in earnest.

"Believe it or not, I've lost my car again," I replied.

"I guess we will have to go back to the precinct," Scott stated.

"Yes, we will," I said as I got out of the car. "I'll be right back." I headed into the pharmacy.

I exited the store with my new medication and hopped back into Scott's car, but I never opened the bottle. The drive to the station was far too fast for me to gain the composure I needed to face what was next.

He parked in front and walked with me again to the main desk. The same gruff woman sat behind the desk, and if she recognized me in any way, she didn't let on. I had a different officer this time, who was rude and perfunctory.

"You're here to get your car, miss?" he asked.

"Yes, I was taken from my car by ambulance to the hospital about ten days ago," I divulged.

"Your car has been impounded," he stated.

Again? I thought to myself. *What the hell?*

"You will have to get it at County Line after you pay the city and state fines and the towing fee," he continued. I knew the County Line drill at that point, but I was unfamiliar with all the other fines and fees.

"Do you take credit cards?" I asked.

"Yes, we take everything," he answered.

I pulled out my Platinum AmEx card and braced myself for the total.

"Fines, fees, and towing come to $2,456," the officer said as he handed me a stack of papers to sign.

Holy crap, I thought. *Am I going to have to pay an additional three grand at County Line?*

The answer in the end was a firm yes. So, including another Uber back to get the car, this escapade of madness had cost me almost $6,000.

Chapter 65
Return to Los Angeles

After picking up my car for the second time at County Line, I drove the distance back to Las Vegas in silence while I tried to make sense of what had happened to me. I couldn't believe what I had been through in the previous weeks, but I didn't have the presence of mind to work through it or make any sense of it.

I stopped at Scott and Deborah's home and picked up my things. Scott got up from his chair under the carport to help me with my luggage.

"Liz, you don't have to leave. You can stay with us longer," Scott said as he lifted my heavy suitcase and multiple bags into the back of my car.

"Thank you, Scott. You have been amazing to me. I don't know how I could ever repay you," I replied. As I hopped into the car, I handed Scott $3,000 cash, approximately what I would have spent at Trump Tower for the same timeframe. "Please, buy good food for Scottie, and do get your headlight fixed."

Scott looked genuinely sad that I was leaving, as I think he really enjoyed the company of an adult who didn't scream at and berate him. I, too, felt a tinge of sadness, for I would miss his friendship, too.

"Let's stay in touch, Liz," he said as I backed out of the chained-in driveway for the last time.

I drove back to Los Angeles without incident, but everything seemed different to me. I no longer saw it as the land of opportunity, and I certainly didn't want to see my son anytime soon. I dragged my large suitcase and stuff from the parking lot to the door of the Airbnb apartment where I was staying. I opened the door with trepidation, not knowing what would greet me.

The apartment was stuffy and hot and smelled like spoiling food. I sat down on the couch and lit a cigarette. The weird thing about this apartment complex was that you were not allowed to smoke outside, just inside, by law. I took full advantage of that fact and chain-smoked for a couple of hours while I planned my next move. In the Nevada psych ward, I had been prescribed medication, but now I didn't feel like I needed it anymore. I took the pills out of my purse, went to the bathroom, and flushed the whole bottle down the toilet. Doing so made me feel that I was in control of my life, not anyone else.

As it was still early in the day, I decided to drive to Malibu, only thirty minutes away on a good day with light traffic. I dressed for the beach in white capri shorts, white tank top, jean jacket, sparkly flip-flops, and a Mercedes baseball cap worn backward.

I drove down Santa Monica Boulevard toward the ocean with a renewed sense of excitement, as I hadn't been to the beach for a long time, or so it seemed in my addled brain. I, like Jerry, had come to believe that the ocean provided certain ions that helped you to feel better.

I stopped at a dispensary and purchased $300 of edibles and flower to share with my surfer friends. My destination was the favored Malibu beach of SoCal surfers, where I had previously made a lot of friends. I had even taken a surfing lesson from one of the dudes. I loved the idea of the surfer's life and had tried to assimilate their lifestyle without being a surfer myself. They seemed to like me, too, or so I thought. In hindsight, I think they just enjoyed my financial gifts, as many surfers seem to live on the edge.

I turned off Santa Monica Boulevard to head north on the US1 to Malibu. As I did, I passed the restaurant where the billionaire had roofied me. It caused an avalanche of emotions, flashbacks, and visceral discomfort. I began to cry as I drove by. I wiped tears from my eyes again as I drove past where I met Jerry less than a year before. All I could see was failure and missed opportunities.

As I headed to the popular surfer beach, I started to hallucinate and marinate in a cesspool of emotions, visions, and broken dreams. My heart felt heavy with all the failure and loss I had been through in my life, much of it caused by my own actions.

After about forty minutes of driving north—enough time to compose myself—I turned left off the road and entered the guarded gate to the beach. Even though the parking lot sign said it was full, the guard recognized me and waved me through without paying. I smiled and waved back at him as I drove through and began to look for a place to park.

Chapter 66
Malibu Beach

This particular Malibu beach is usually filled with the same group of surfers seven days a week—about twenty-five of them—who congregate to surf and party. On this day, though, I didn't see the usual crew. The parking lot was filled with tourists and people I didn't recognize. I didn't find a parking space, so I double-parked in front of an empty police car and hopped out on the sandy pavement. It seemed completely appropriate to do so.

I walked a few yards to the beach and took a seat near the water. On the horizon, there were several large boats. This was not a common sight in Malibu, as there are no boat launches in the city. I began to hallucinate and see things. I also heard the roar of a close helicopter but couldn't see it. My old delusions soon joined me, and my mind began to create a story about the boats and the helicopter. I truly believed my sons were waving to me from one of the boats and Elon Musk was in the approaching helicopter. I thought Elon would pick me up in the helicopter on the beach and take me to my boys on the yacht, where we would all embark on a cruise together. I started to get excited about the new adventure I believed was unfolding for me.

Soon enough, my delusions and hallucinations were interrupted by one of my surfer friends, Chris. He approached me and asked, "Hey, Liz! What are you doing here?"

"I'm here to see you guys," I replied.

"Awesome. Do you want to come to my van?" he asked.

"Sure," I said as he helped me up from the sand.

This surfer was a mixed bag for me, so I wasn't thrilled to be hanging out with him, but I hoped he would take me to the other guys I liked better. On a prior visit to California, I had believed that I had the unique ability to heal animals from any affliction. I also had believed I was a dog whisperer of sorts and could miraculously cause a bad or ill-tempered dog to become docile. I had tested this theory with Chris' menacing mutt and managed to get a big dog bite on my face from the little shit. Although my wound had healed, the scars from that bite still made me apprehensive about hanging out with him.

I joined Chris in his van, where his dog sat and growled at me. I marveled at how similar all the surfer vans were: multiple boards dominating the scene; a requisite makeshift bed; wetsuits hanging from every corner; some sort of cob-jobbed stereo and/or television; and, of course, Bob Marley albums and marijuana paraphernalia.

Chris loaded a pipe and offered me the first hit of the pot I had brought to the beach. On this particular day, I wasn't feeling like imbibing, so I politely declined while handing him another bud from the flower purchase I had made.

"Where's everyone else?" I asked.

"They're all at a surfing competition in Ventura," he replied.

"Oh, I see," I said as I realized I had been gone from Los Angeles for quite a while and hadn't kept up on the activities of my new friends.

Just then, my phone rang. I looked at the phone and was relieved to learn it was a good friend calling. "Chris, I need to take this call," I said as I gathered up my things and hopped out of the van.

"Thanks for the bud, Liz!" Chris shouted behind me.

I answered the phone as I walked to my car. "Hi, Carl."

"Hey, Liz!" he replied. "Can you come up to Santa Barbara tomorrow? There are some exciting developments that I'd like to discuss with you."

Carl was someone I had met in my hometown of Seattle, but he hailed from SoCal and was essentially Hollywood royalty. He is a screenwriter and very active in all things in the entertainment world. For years, we would visit each other whenever I was in Los Angeles or he was in Seattle. We hadn't seen each other in a while, and he had recently moved to Santa Barbara. Carl and I had talked about writing and producing a movie together, and would meet often for brainstorming sessions.

"Yes, I can come up tomorrow," I answered.

"Awesome!" he replied. "Meet me at the Four Seasons at ten o'clock for coffee. I have an executive producer who is going to join us to talk about your project," he replied, referencing a book I was writing about my medical career. "This guy comes with the money, too, and just might be the perfect partner for our screenplay."

"Sounds great. I can't wait. See you then," I finished.

I decided to go back to the beach and see if the boat and my sons were still there. They were.

The boat appeared much closer to shore, and I swore I could see the details of my sons' faces, even though they were still far away. Likewise, the sounds of the helicopter got louder and louder until I saw it crest over the mountain behind me. It was flying low as it approached the sandy beach to land to my right. Sand was showered everywhere by the massive rotors, causing most of the beachgoers to flee. I was convinced that the helicopter, complete with Elon—was landing to pick me up, so I stayed in the sand blast and shielded my face.

The helicopter made several attempts to land on the sand but then pulled away and did not return. I was crestfallen and sure that I would never see my sons, or Elon, ever again. The boat that had seemed so close just a little bit ago now seemed impossibly far in the distance. I truly believed that my life was over. I began to weep and placed my head in my hands as the tears flowed.

Chapter 67
Four Seasons, Santa Barbara

After a while on the beach and as the sun set, I decided to move on. Given that I had a meeting planned in Santa Barbara in the morning and I was already an hour closer than where I was staying in West Los Angeles, I decided to head straight to Santa Barbara for the night. I hadn't prepared for this meeting with Carl and only had the clothes on my back and hundreds of dollars of marijuana with me. I decided I could shop in Santa Barbara if I needed anything and assumed I would have no problem getting a hotel room.

As I headed north on US1, I began to feel more and more disconnected from reality. I tried to keep myself alert as I brushed tears from my face. I suddenly had a profound sense of doom and danger come over me, and I became fearful of my trip to Santa Barbara—rather than excited—for unknown reasons. Although I was desperate to be with another human being, I didn't have the presence of mind to call my friend back in Santa Barbara and ask to stay with him. I thought I had to survive the night all alone.

I arrived in Santa Barbara after dark and drove straight to the Four Seasons, having been there before. As I approached the entrance, several guards were blocking the entrance. I rolled down my window and confidently approached the closest guard.

"Hi. I'm checking in for the night. I have a meeting here tomorrow morning," I said to the guard.

"Sorry, miss, we are closed to the public tonight. There is a private party taking place," he replied.

"I believe that I am supposed to be at that party," I said confidently.

"Who is the party host?" the guard asked.

"Oprah," I replied without hesitation. I knew she lived in this town, and it seemed so logical to think she was the one tying up the property.

"May I have your name, please?" he inquired.

I handed him my business card, and he took it back to the guard shack. I watched him pick up the phone and read my name to the person on the other end. The guard hung up the phone and approached my car.

"You are not on the guest list, miss," he stated. "I'm very sorry, but you'll have to leave."

I decided not to press the issue and backed up and turned around. I decided to drive around town for a while to figure out what to do next. I found another hotel and tried to get a room, but got into it with the very rude front desk guy when he told me the only room he had available was $800 per night.

I left that hotel and decided to go back to the Four Seasons and give it a second try. This time, the guards were disbursed, and the entrance was unmanned. I turned into the long, winding driveway and stopped under the porte cochere in front of the hotel. I looked inside the entrance and saw no one. No activity, no people, nothing. At that moment, I failed to see why I couldn't get a room for the night.

As I prepared to exit my car and head inside, I heard a loud knock on my window. I looked up to see a security guard staring directly at me. I panicked, hit the accelerator, and gave a little wave as I exited the property as quickly but still as normally as I could.

Chapter 68

Uh-Oh

Back on the main road, I drove past the perimeter of the hotel complex and parking lot. I saw a vacant driveway about one hundred yards away, adjacent to the hotel and pulled into it. I sat in my car for a few minutes and tried to collect my thoughts. I figured I could just sleep in my car at that point and go to the meeting with Carl and the Hollywood producer the next day.

I decided to play music on my car's incredible sound system and wait for sleep to take over. About thirty minutes later, there was another knock on my window, this time from a policeman with guns around his waist. I got out of the car and was surrounded by three cop cars and six uniformed men.

"What are you doing here, miss?" the closest police officer asked.

"I'm here for a meeting," I replied.

"At nine o'clock at night?" he continued.

"The meeting is in the morning. I'm just looking for a place to stay," I replied.

The cop simultaneously motioned for me to step away from the car and instructed his colleagues to search it. "We're going to need to do a sobriety test, miss," the cop said to me as I watched the others tear up my car.

"Okay," I said as I began to focus on his instructions for the test. At first, the exercises were simple, but quickly they became impossible by anyone, drunk or sober.

"Sir, no one could pass that test you're asking me to do, even if they were sober, which I am!" I said after watching him try to show me what to do. He couldn't even do it himself!

The cop smiled and turned to his mates and said, "You know she is right!"

The sobriety test quickly deteriorated, and the cop seemed satisfied with his assessment—and my reassurances—that I was not drunk. The kind of impairment I had at that time would not be easily determined by standard sobriety tests.

"We are going to need to take your car, miss," the cop said.

"Why?" I asked incredulously.

"It's a technicality, really, but you can pick it up here next week," he replied.

I was in no condition to fight with a cop, so I acquiesced and got back out of the car and handed the cop the keys.

"Do you need a ride anywhere?" the cop asked.

"No, I'll call a Lyft," I said.

I pulled out my phone and ordered a limo from Lyft. Somehow, just a plain car just didn't seem right, but a limo seemed perfect. The app asked me where I was going, of course, so I decided to enter LAX, completely forgetting about my meeting with Carl the next morning in Santa Barbara.

"We will stay with you until your car arrives," the cop said.

I was both happy and not so happy about this development. "Thank you," I replied as I stood next to my car.

Chapter 69
Goodbye, Santa Barbara

We waited for what seemed like forever for my ride to arrive. When it did, a beat-up, old car arrived with a scary-looking driver behind the wheel.

"Are you comfortable, miss?" the cop asked as I walked toward the dilapidated car.

"I'll be fine, sir," I replied as I opened the door. Once inside, I asked the driver, "How come a limo didn't come? That's what I ordered on the app."

"Lady, if you're too good for this car, you can just get out now," he replied.

I had a choice to wait longer with the cops for another ride or continue with this most unpleasant driver. I decided to proceed to LAX to the private plane I was newly convinced was waiting for me.

I shut the door behind me to the Lyft and said goodbye to my car and the cops. I wasn't worried about my present situation and figured it would all work out in the end. I had my sights set at that point on going to LAX and taking a private plane with Tony Robbins to his private island in the South Pacific. At this point, my delusions and hallucinations were fast and furious, and my plans changed at whim based on what I was seeing/hearing/experiencing in my mind at that moment.

I turned my attention to the driver. He was relatively young, foreign, and clearly in a very bad mood. *Perhaps he resented my long trip? Maybe he didn't like women?* I didn't know, but it didn't take us long to get into an argument about which way to go to LAX. Our ride became increasingly hostile, and the driver made several derogatory remarks about Americans, and women in particular. I was not comfortable at all with this driver and asked him to stop at a store so I could get something to drink and figure out my next move.

We stopped in Oxnard at a convenience store. I went inside to get a kombucha, and when I exited the store, I realized the car and driver were gone. Fortunately, I hadn't left anything in the car. I sat down on the curb in front of the store and began to cry again. I cupped my face in my hands and felt like I had reached the end of my rope. I believed I was out of ideas and options. It still never occurred to me to call Carl in Santa Barbara or anyone else.

I eventually got up and walked behind the store into another parking lot. I saw a car that looked a lot like mine, and I truly believed it was my car waiting for me. I was so disoriented at that point. I approached the car and discovered the door unlocked and the keys in the center console. The car's interior also looked familiar with the same gear shift as mine, so I didn't think twice about driving away in my altered state of mind.

At that point, I had decided on a psychic whim that the better airport to meet up with Tony Robbins was now Ventura, not LAX. I turned onto the freeway and headed east toward Ventura. It was a long drive for my impaired state and sleep deprivation. I soon dozed off behind the wheel, traveling at seventy-five miles per hour, and was jolted awake when another car honked furiously at me as I was careening toward a cement wall. I woke up in a panic and realized I was about to crash head-on into my certain death. I violently grabbed the steering wheel and narrowly avoided what probably would have been my untimely demise.

Chapter 70

A Visit to Ventura

The near-accident occurred just a few miles out of the city, and I made it to the Ventura airport without any more near-misses, albeit shaking like a leaf. I decided to valet the car, just as I had done hundreds of times back home at the airport in Seattle. I gathered my things in the car, handed the keys to the valet, and confidently walked into the airport.

Once there, I realized I had left something in the car, so I headed back to the valet. I took the keys from him, got what I needed in the car, and turned back to go inside. I knew I needed to find Tony Robbins' plane, so I approached the nearest ticket counter to ask the absurd question about his whereabouts. As I did, a uniformed and armed police officer approached me. He seemed pleasant and was smiling at me.

"Hello, miss. I am Officer Warren. I need you to come with me," he said as the smile left his face.

I was terribly embarrassed as we walked together to their offices in the airport, but forever grateful in 20/20 hindsight that he hadn't put me in handcuffs. I had no idea why he wanted to talk to me, as I was unaware in my altered state, I had driven someone else's car.

I entered the office, and Officer Warren motioned for me to have a seat. "We've received an all-points bulletin about a stolen car, and guess what car just arrived at the airport with you behind the wheel?" he asked me with a smirk on his face.

I truly had no idea what he was talking about and told him so. This did not help my situation at all.

"We've reviewed the camera footage at the valet, and you were definitely the driver," he finished.

"What happens now?" I asked, still not understanding what had happened.

"We are going to ask you a few questions, and we will let you know what happens next," he replied.

This did not sound encouraging, and I braced myself for the worst, an arrest … again.

I spent a couple of hours with the cops at Ventura airport and tried my best to negotiate with them to let me leave and go back to Los Angeles. I did share with them, however, my deep connection to Tony Robbins, Elon Musk, and Steve Jobs. They seemed to be amused at my endless chatter and tall tales, which I hoped would help the situation I was in.

The police contacted the owners of the car, who declined to press charges against me. I thought this was my ticket to freedom. It wasn't.

"Well, Liz, we are going to have to arrest you," Officer Warren finally stated.

My heart sank as I realized the significance of a misdemeanor charge and what was happening.

"Come with me," a different cop said as he handcuffed my wrists behind my back. I rode in the rear of his car with my hands trapped behind my back against a hard, plastic seat, a very uncomfortable thing to do if you haven't tried it.

The drive to the jail was long and hot, but highly amusing as I watched the cop work on his laptop computer and phone while driving eighty-five miles per hour all the way to the jail.

As opposed to when I was arrested after being roofied, this time I was fully awake and drug-free, albeit manic, for the intake proceedings. It was, and remains, one of the worst experiences of my life. If you haven't been in jail before, I don't recommend it.

The building was huge and sterile. I was taken to the intake/booking area where I was roughly searched, photographed, fingerprinted, and booked, all while being manhandled and screamed at by a morbidly obese, heinous woman, her vast flesh hanging out from a poorly tucked, too-small shirt and pants.

When not participating in one of those activities, I was told to face the cement wall with my hands above my head and legs spread, threatened with violence if I did not comply. It was, and is, a completely degrading experience. I believe working in a jail or prison was a job that no sane person would want. It truly brings out the worst in all involved.

My stay in the slammer was far too long for my broken body and psyche. Without the ability to roam freely and distract myself with movement or electronics, the days were interminable and the nights torturous. My hallucinations and delusions—which had occasionally provided me with amusement and purpose— now turned completely dark, scary, and foreboding around the clock.

I was placed in a tiny metal and cement cell. I had a roommate who was actively withdrawing from something who spent her time writhing and screaming around the clock. The facility was freezing with air-conditioning blasting the cells 24/7. Each inmate was given a tiny, threadbare blanket and no pillow, which did little to warm me up. I trembled with cold and goosebumps the entire time I was in the facility.

While in jail, I had terrifying hallucinations by daylight and foreboding nightmares by dark. I visualized the United States being attacked and destroyed via an air/land/sea assault by China. This was not a common concern of the general public at that time, so these thoughts seemed outrageous, but I did (and still do) think this could be a real concern. I also foresaw Russia and China joining forces against us, an unthinkable partnership at that time, which only heightened my anxiety in jail.

There was a common area for the inmates, which was an openly hostile and an actively dangerous place to be. There were about fifty women in this area of the facility, and the group was ruled by a duo of young black women who controlled us with verbal intimidation, threats of violence, and promises of sexual assault. We complied.

Jail is a place where wills are broken and adherence to the rules is mandatory if you don't want to exacerbate your situation. You are also on edge twenty-four hours a day due to the constant risk of violence. If you want to shower, you must have money wired to you by someone on the outside so you can purchase soap and shampoo. You are not granted access to the showers unless you have your own toiletries. But with fifty women and one phone in the common area, it was impossible to reach anyone in my life to ask for funds for grooming. So, I marinated in the orange scrubs for the duration of my stay.

Food in jail is really a misnomer. While we were given meals three times a day, it was generally inedible. Baked beans, bare hot dogs, and a slice of white bread were two of the daily meals, with breakfast consisting only of milk and a piece of white bread. Despite its low quality, food was often used as a bargaining tool in the jail, with the two obese matriarchs demanding food from those of us considered more vulnerable and under their influence. It was shocking how much violence, intimidation, and harassment among each other by the inmates is allowed in jails. While incarceration may protect those on the outside, it is a very violent environment inside, and the wardens did not seem to care as they watched us from above in their perch overlooking the common area. It was a very high testosterone environment, even with only biological women in the jail at that time.

A few days after admission, I thankfully went before a judge and was released with my case dismissed. As I was exiting the courtroom in my orange outfit, I heard the judge say to my state-assigned lawyer, "Don't worry. She'll be back."

I truly felt I had hit rock bottom.

Chapter 71
Los Angeles, Again

Upon release, the Ventura jail gave me a bus ticket to LAX. They didn't, however, tell me how to get to the bus, and I was unceremoniously released back into society. Somehow, I had lost my phone and wallet—again—somewhere between the convenience store and the Ventura airport. I exited the jail and looked around me. Here I was in another strange city without the means to function normally. I thought about hitchhiking, but thought better of that idea.

I walked the streets of Ventura aimlessly in the scorching heat for several hours before I summoned up the courage to ask a bus driver how to get to the bus station.

"Hop in. I'm going that way," the driver said.

"But I don't have any money for a fare," I replied.

"Get in, lady. I won't charge you," he finished as he reached for the door lever.

I climbed the stairs up into the bus and said, "Thank you, sir," before sitting down near the front.

The driver eventually stopped the bus and said, "The bus station is over there," while pointing to it across the street. I thanked him profusely, exited the bus, and walked in the scorching sun to the station. It seemed enormous and very confusing to me.

In my fragile condition, it took me over an hour to find the bus to LAX, and when I did, I learned I had just missed it. The next one was over two hours away, so I decided to get some food, but had forgotten that I had no money.

I placed an order at a fast-food restaurant in the station and then ran away empty-handed before I was required to pay. I was very hungry, as I hadn't eaten much while in jail because the food was disgusting. I contemplated eating food that others had discarded at the bus station, but thought the better of that option. Instead, I decided to look for lost money and change on the ground.

I walked the perimeter of the station and found quite a few coins and a dollar bill. I eventually had enough money to get a Snickers, which I ate on the bus to Los Angeles. The bus ride was long and hot, and I wondered if the other riders could tell I had just been released from jail. I felt self-conscious and emotionally naked. We eventually got to LAX, and I hopped out of the bus to figure out my next move.

The apartment where I was staying in West Los Angeles wasn't too far away from LAX, but was way too far to walk. As I didn't want to call my son for help, I borrowed a stranger's phone and called a friend in London on WhatsApp. It was the middle of the night for him, but he still answered the phone.

"Hi, Steven. It's Liz. I'm terribly sorry to call you at this hour," I said.

"Hello, Liz! Are you okay?" he asked, sounding surprised to hear from me in the middle of his night.

"Actually, I'm in need of some help," I replied.

"Whatever you need, Liz, I got you," he replied.

"I'm at LAX and need an Uber to where I am staying in West Los Angeles," I stated, trying to sound like what I had just said would be enough to curry a favor from a friend.

"I've got you," he replied. "Just tell me where you're at, and I'll call one for you."

"I'm at the Bradley Terminal," I replied.

"You'll be at your place soon, Liz," he said, reassuring me without any knowledge of what had just happened to me.

I was ever so grateful that he didn't ask me why I needed him to order an Uber and transferred him the funds as soon as I got back to the apartment.

I got back to the Airbnb and entered the same neglected apartment. I sat on the couch, lit a cigarette, and pondered my situation. My first cigarette in freedom was divine. But the optimism and energy I had when I visited Southern California for the first time about a year before was now gone, replaced by interminable pain and misery. Rather than finding a better situation in California, I found I had simply brought my Washington misery with me.

My money was running short, and I wasn't feeling my best anymore physically. My weight loss was now becoming a concern for my family and friends. I was unsure of how to change or improve my situation. I decided that I needed to clean up my stuff in the apartment and began what would be several hours of mayhem.

I believed at that time all my possessions I had brought with me to or acquired in Los Angeles and Las Vegas each contained a vibration. Now, I think that this might be an actual scientific fact, but at that moment, each item I owned was vibrating with either a positive or negative energy. I was able to tell instantly when I touched an object whether it was there to help or hurt me. If an item were there to help, I felt nothing when I touched it, and it went into one pile on the carpet. If it were there to hurt me, as exemplified by a static electricity-type sensation when I touched it, it would be disposed of.

I literally handled every single item in the apartment, including food, and made piles in each room. When done—and with every worldly possession on the floor or counter—I was proud of the work and felt like I had accomplished a very important task. It looked like a bomb had gone off in the apartment.

I thought about going out to Malibu, but had totally forgotten I no longer had a car. Instead, I decided to stay in the apartment, walking to the convenience store when I needed something.

I spent several erratic and generally sleepless days and nights, holed up in the increasingly chaotic environment inside the apartment. I spent hours on the computer watching YouTube videos that seemed to be curated just for me. I had little need for food or sleep, and I subsisted mostly on yogurt, coffee, and Perrier. I began to lose touch with reality, and the days and nights became indistinguishable.

Being alone in the apartment was not good for me, but I was too ill to ask for help. My world got smaller and smaller with each passing day, and I became more and more out of touch with reality. My son apparently tried to contact me several times, but I missed his messages.

Chapter 72

Charity

One morning after a fitful three-hour sleep, I decided it was time to share my bounty. I dressed up in black ripped jeans, black flip-flops, a white cami, and a black jean jacket. I stuffed my vintage Louis Vuitton purse with crisp $100 bills and headed to Santa Monica Boulevard.

Once there, I searched for anyone I could find who appeared homeless. I noticed a few people with shopping carts sitting at a bus stop. I crossed the street and took a seat between an elderly man with no teeth and a younger black woman who appeared to be tweaking. I introduced myself and asked them how I could help them.

"We need money!" the old man said in reply.

"I just want a bed to sleep on," the younger woman added.

We chatted a bit more, and I quickly pulled out two $100 bills from my purse. I slowly handed a bill to each of them and laughed as they marveled at their good fortune. The woman kissed the money, leaned over, and gave me a big, awkward hug. The older man started crying and called to his friends a few feet away. Soon, I was surrounded by ten or so homeless people, all asking for their own $100 bill.

I emptied my purse of the $1,000 I had brought with me and hugged each recipient before I returned to the apartment. It felt good to give something of myself, and it was great to see the joy on their faces. I vowed to continue to help the homeless in any way I could.

Chapter 73
Neighbor Joe

One night as I was smoking on the deck of the apartment (an illegal activity, as I should have been smoking inside,) a new neighbor appeared out of nowhere and introduced himself. "Hi. I'm Joe," he said as he held out his hand.

"Hi, Joe. I'm Liz," I replied as I shook his hand.

"Can I bum a cigarette from you?" he asked.

"Sure, here you go," I replied while handing him the pack and a lighter.

"Where do you live?" I asked.

"I'm right here." He gestured to the door next to my Airbnb. "Just moved in today. I'm renting while my house gets built."

Joe was quite handsome and appeared to be about thirty years old. After we finished our cigarette, he invited me to join him at a party he was hosting the following night in his apartment. I was grateful for the activity and opportunity to socialize.

"I'd love to. Thank you so much," I replied.

"Awesome! Come over at eight o'clock," he said as he turned around and disappeared into his apartment.

The next day, I dressed casually in a white sundress and flat sandals and arrived at the party on time. I knocked on the door, and Joe let me in and gave me a hug hello, signaling a familiarity that wasn't yet established, especially in standoffish Los Angeles. There were only a few people there, and most of them were working on their laptops.

Although it was ostensibly a housewarming party (albeit in an apartment), there was no food or drink anywhere visible. The only things I could see on the tables were drugs and drug paraphernalia. But these drugs were not the surfer's marijuana type. They were seriously hard drugs, which made me feel instantly uncomfortable. Meth, cocaine, crack, and more were laid out on the tables carelessly. The guests who were working on their computers were snorting lines and freebasing. The only person who I didn't see doing drugs was Joe, the host.

Joe and I sat on the couch together and started to exchange stories. I told him I was not doing well—physically, emotionally, or financially—and was struggling in life. He listened intently and said he would like to help me. He told me he was a businessman and was related to royalty in Ireland, where he was from, and showed me pictures of his family's castle in Dublin. He further said he had a trust fund and didn't have to worry about money. He showed me some schematics of his mansion being built in Malibu, and I wondered how and why he had picked the modest apartment complex where he was now. In my friable state, I started to trust him, without any apparent reason to do so.

Joe asked me lots of questions about my life and even asked me if I had an American Express card, which seemed like a random question. I told him I had a Platinum AmEx, and he showed me his own. He said he thought people who had Platinum AmEx cards were better people, which sounded like a weird qualifier for goodness in people. In hindsight, I overlooked one red flag after another, but I was too ill to make a prescient analysis of my situation.

After about an hour and before the pizza and sodas arrived, I got up and let Joe know that I needed to go back to my place and get some rest. Over the next few days, Joe and I continued to hang out and developed what I thought was a genuine friendship. Little did I know he had other plans for our association.

Chapter 74
Circling the Drain

The next morning, after my usual coffee and cigarette, I felt an incredible sense of danger and fear. I believed that some of the world's most powerful people were after me and saw me as a threat to their businesses and wanted me eliminated, despite no objective evidence to substantiate my paranoia. I tried to settle down by chain-smoking, to no avail. I finally decided I needed to call the police to have them take care of my tormentors. I placed a call to 911.

"911, what is your emergency?" the man asked.

"I'm being chased by some really rich men who want me dead," I replied.

"Where are you, miss?" he asked.

"I'm in an apartment, but they are coming to get me!" I responded excitedly.

"Help is on its way. Stay with me on the phone until the police arrive," he instructed.

"I will," I said as I started to hear sirens in the distance.

A few minutes later, the fire truck arrived first. The firefighters came up to the door and asked me to step outside.

"What seems to be the problem, miss?" an impossibly handsome fireman asked me.

"I am being hunted by some of the world's wealthiest men," I replied.

"And who would that be?" he asked, trying to remain serious and avoid smiling, looking around at the modest apartment building.

"It's not just one; it's *all* of them," I stated.

By that time, about fifteen people—EMS, fire, and police—were all surrounding me in front of the apartment door. I had been surrounded by EMS before, and I didn't want to be trapped again, like in Las Vegas. Further, I didn't want my new friend and neighbor, Joe, to see me in this current situation.

"I'm sorry. I shouldn't have called. I'll be fine. I just need some sleep," I blurted to defuse the situation.

"Are you sure you don't want to come with us?" an ambulance driver asked.

"No, thank you," I replied.

One of the paramedics stepped forward and said, "Liz, we need to check you out. Can we go inside?"

"Of course," I replied and turned around to open the door.

What a sight it must have been for the uninitiated and sound of mind. The floors were not visible under the mess of piles I had created in the preceding days. Stuff was strewn everywhere, and what was a modestly nice apartment had been turned into a junkyard.

The paramedic followed me inside and sat with me on the couch. He took my blood pressure, pulse, and oxygen saturation and listened to my lungs.

"Everything seems okay," he said to his colleagues peeking in through the door behind him.

I felt relieved I was okay, but mortified that I was the object of their curiosity and prolonged attention.

"Well, Liz, I guess we will leave it here. Please call us back if you need us," he said as he stood to leave.

"Thank you. I will," I said as he closed the door behind him.

I went back to my computer and lit a cigarette, feeling embarrassed that I had dialed 911. I continued to watch a selection of videos curated just for me, or so I thought. The messages from YouTube became more and more bizarre and threatening to my safety. Most troubling, I learned that Mark Zuckerberg had apparently stolen my patented formulas for my Seattle skincare company and was making a fortune off my intellectual property and patents. Of course, none of my delusions were true, but these scared the hell out of me and couldn't have been more real.

After a few more hours of mindful torture, I couldn't take it anymore, so I dialed 911 again. This time, the cops didn't come, but

EMS and the fire crew did. As they knocked on my door for the second time, I instantly regretted calling them. I felt I should have been able to handle my life without the aid of others. We had a brief conversation, after which they all left again.

Chapter 75
Jimmy Again

I didn't want to stay inside any longer, so I decided to walk down to the convenience store and get something to drink. For the short walk and outing, I packed up a Birkin bag with $5,000 cash and a few pieces of my favorite jewelry, along with a few other notable items. I included the only bottle of perfume I had developed for one of my companies and a few other important mementos, including my passport.

I changed into clean clothes and fixed my hair and makeup for the short walk to the corner store. I wore white ripped jeans, a lace cami, vintage jean jacket, and a pair of low but strappy sandals. I literally thought it was possible that I might run into Elon (I knew he lived nearby the apartment), so I wanted to look good and be prepared for the potential face-to-face meeting.

I was tired, very tired. My body was beat up and weary from my time in jail, and I just wanted out—out of my situation, out of my career, and out of my life. To distract myself from contemplating suicide again, I decided to roam the streets of Santa Monica on foot.

As I rounded the corner to the store, I was met by Jimmy sitting at the bus stop in front of the convenience store.

"Hey, Liz!" he exclaimed.

"Hi, Jimmy," I replied as I sat down next to him, happy to see someone I knew.

"Liz, you really are a beautiful woman," he said.

"Why, thank you, Jimmy. I haven't heard that from anyone in a long time," I replied with a smile. "I need to get something to drink. Will you watch my purse?" I asked illogically as I stood to my feet and left my purse on the bus stop bench.

"Of course! It's safe with me, Liz," Jimmy replied.

I will never know why I decided to leave my Birkin bag with Jimmy, but I did. I went into the store and grabbed a kombucha, the official drink of Los Angeles, I think. I stood in line to pay, and when I reached the counter, I noticed that the lottery was over $100 million. I had stuffed a couple hundred dollars into my jeans, and now that I was paying for my drink, I decided it was a good time to purchase lottery tickets.

I turned to the line of people behind me in the store, about fifteen of them, and bought them all lottery tickets. I then held up my ticket and declared that we all would be the winner of the jackpot. There was a celebratory atmosphere in the store, and I felt ebullient at the thought of my winnings and how I would disperse it all to my charities that were formed in my head.

I exited the store and headed back to the bus stop. I searched for Jimmy and my purse, but they were nowhere to be found. A couple of new people were now at the bus stop, so I asked each one of them if they had seen my purse or Jimmy. No one seemed to know what I was talking about, and all claimed innocence. I truly thought I was going to lose it completely at that point and ran away from the area screaming at the top of my lungs. I slowed as I got near the apartment and began to cry. *How could I have been so dumb? Why am I such an idiot? Why did I leave my purse with Jimmy? Why did I trust him?*

I had no answers, just questions for myself.

Unfortunately, no enlightenment was forthcoming from the recesses of my mind, and I was left with utter despondent thoughts. Suicide seemed a pretty good option at that point.

Chapter 76

Descent into Darkness

I let myself back into the apartment, thankful I had kept the keys in my pocket. I was furious at the thought of what I had lost, including the Birkin bag, $5,000 cash, my passport, my perfume, my new iPhone, and my pride. Without any forethought, I decided to call 911 again from a second phone that I owned. *This might be the worst decision of my life or the best*, I thought to myself. Only time would tell.

I sat on the couch smoking as I heard the approaching sirens. This time, only the firefighters came to the door. I opened the door before they could knock.

"Hi, Liz. What's going on?" the man asked me, somewhat wearily, but still professional.

"I don't know. I just feel like I am going to die," I replied.

"Okay, Liz, as this is our third visit to see you today, you now have a choice," he said. "Come with us to the hospital, or go with the police to jail," he said matter-of-factly.

"Can't I just stay here?" I pleaded in a soft voice, clenching my fists in fear of what could transpire next.

"Maybe if you hadn't called us three times today," he replied. "Now, you don't have the choice of staying here anymore."

I knew I was in trouble and absolutely didn't want to go back to jail. "I'll go with you guys," I replied to the EMS with my head in my hands.

"Good decision," he finished. He then talked into his walkie-talkie and indicated I had chosen the hospital over another arrest.

Before I left, I let Joe know that I was going to the hospital. I gathered a few things from the trashed apartment and followed the fire chief out of the complex onto the street. I didn't, however, have the presence of mind to put on shoes.

Once streetside, an ambulance awaited me. The EMS helped me into the vehicle and waved goodbye to the firefighters as we pulled out into traffic. Two very good-looking men were in the back of the ambulance with me, and we chatted about politics, the weather, and my good friends, Steve Jobs and Elon Musk.

"Where are we going?" I finally asked one of them.

"University of California, Los Angeles (UCLA) Hospital Emergency Room," he replied.

UCLA? Oh shit! I thought. That's where my son works, along with a few of my own friends and former physician colleagues.

"Do we *have* to go there?" I asked.

"Yes, they've agreed to take you," the EMS replied.

Geez, that sounds so inviting, I thought to myself, wondering what lay ahead for me.

Truthfully, I don't remember much after that moment. I recall waking up in the emergency department, having frank delusions and hallucinations. I was crying at the top of my lungs, thrashing beneath the four-point restraints, convinced I was most assuredly heading to my imminent death at the hands of UCLA. I stayed in the emergency room for over forty-eight hours before I was assigned a bed in their psych ward. I had never been there before, and my only frame of reference was haunting memories from my time in the horrendous Nevada psychiatric ward.

Chapter 77
UCLA Psychiatric Ward

I woke up in the UCLA psychiatric ward to bright sunshine streaming through my window. I was in a single room, which is rare for most psych wards. I was hungry, *really* hungry, and couldn't remember the last time I had eaten. A nurse came into my room and introduced himself and asked if I would like some food. After I said yes, he disappeared and returned a few minutes later with the requisite psychiatric snack: graham crackers, peanut butter, and cranberry juice. It felt like home, as this was the exact snack I used to eat when I would admit patients to the psych ward during residency.

I was given scrubs to change into and a handful of toiletries so I could take a shower. I tried to relax as the lukewarm water trickled down my body from my head to my toes. Very disoriented, I searched my mind for any memory of how I got there and came up blank.

When I was done with my shower, I dressed in the hospital scrubs and poked my head into the hallway. I didn't see anyone, so I went back to bed and fell asleep. The next time I woke up, it was morning. I realized I had missed dinner the night before, and again, I was very hungry. I ran a comb through my hair and brushed my teeth before venturing out into the hallway. Of note, UCLA psych ward bathrooms have mirrors!

The psychiatric ward at UCLA is truly one of the best. I had an incredible care team and was treated with amazing respect, given the mental state I was in at that time. The food, which is generally terrible in hospitals, was nutritious and delicious. The activities were mostly artistic in nature and quite soothing for my splintered soul. We, the fractured inmates, were treated with the utmost respect and kindness.

I can honestly say that it was here at UCLA that my healing began. As the days passed, my mind became clearer and clearer as my body began to repair itself. I ate a lot of good food and began to feel comfortable putting a little weight back on my emaciated frame. Medication was prescribed, and I took it willingly. I knew one thing for certain: I could not continue in the state I was in when I was admitted. It had become clear to me that my death would not be far away unless I got help.

Finally, after two weeks, my discharge day arrived, and I was released with a new sense of optimism. I decided to go from the hospital to a facility in Malibu to continue my healing. The hospital arranged an Uber for me, which I took to Malibu. The driver was very chatty and clearly didn't know I had just been discharged from the loony bin. He asked me lots of questions about my life, to which I really didn't know what to say in reply.

Liz Casper

"Hi, I'm Liz. I'm a fuck-up from Seattle, visiting Los Angeles trying—and failing—to make a new life for myself" really didn't have a catchy ring to it, so I mostly remained quiet and gave one-word answers to his probing questions. I did, however, ask him to stop at my favorite gas station in Malibu, where I knew they carried the cigarettes I liked.

Chapter 78
A Place to Heal in Malibu

The drive to Malibu from UCLA was long and hot. We inched our way through tons of traffic and headed up PCH to the northern, private part of Malibu. Again, we passed the restaurant where I had been roofied, the spot where I met Jerry, the beach where I thought I was meeting Elon and my sons, and so forth. Memories—some good, some very bad—flashed through my mind as we passed each one. I felt an incredible sense of loss and humiliation, realizing that I hadn't accomplished much of anything in all my visits to Los Angeles and Las Vegas, except my own destruction.

As we left the public area of Malibu and headed north, the traffic thinned out, and we neared my next destination.

"Almost there, miss," the driver said as he pulled off PCH and into a fancy neighborhood with a guarded gate.

Driving up to the place that would become my home for the next month was incredible. The facility was a converted mansion once owned by one of the music industry's biggest stars, with all the glitz and glamour still intact. The front door opened as I walked up the marble stairs, and a beautiful young woman greeted me.

"Welcome to paradise, Liz," she said as she grabbed the hospital bags from my hands.

When I arrived at UCLA, I only had the clothes on my back and no shoes. UCLA provided me with a complete change of clothes and shoes from their donation closet, made possible by wealthy benefactors and volunteers. What few things were given to me at UCLA were the only items I had when I arrived in Malibu. In contrast, most of the other wealthy residents of this facility had planned their stay there and had arrived with packed Louis Vuitton luggage. I felt like a poor stepchild with my donated hand-me-downs, but tried to rock the clothes as much as I could.

I stepped through the door in my UCLA psych ward flip-flops (which I still have to this day), and the home and its decor stopped me in my tracks.

"Holy crap! This place is incredible," I exclaimed to the woman as I looked around the interior of the mansion.

"Yes, it is. This is a center for healing and transformation. Follow me. I'll take you to your room," she said as she began to walk.

I walked behind her and felt the stares of other residents that accompany any new addition to a close-knit community, such as at this center.

We walked through gorgeous gardens with stunning views of the Pacific Ocean. There were waterfalls, koi ponds, a putting green, sparkling pools, and flowers and foliage that were out of this world. She eventually arrived at another home on the property where my room was.

"You lucked out, Liz. You got a single room," she said as she put my bags on the bed.

Thank God for that, I thought as I acknowledged to myself that I was in no condition to socialize or make small talk. The room was luxurious, and the bathroom incredible.

"We are just about to have dinner, so please come back up to the main house as soon as you can," she said as she left.

I sat down on the bed and noticed the luxurious linens and down pillows as compared to the rubber-clad pillow and mattress in psych wards. I let out a big sigh of relief and congratulated myself for making it this far. I freshened up with a quick shower and walked back to the manor house for dinner.

When I reached the manor house, I saw a large, beautiful outdoor table filled with people already eating. I saw one empty seat next to a handsome man with long, rock-star hair.

"May I sit here?" I asked as I approached the table.

"Of course. What's your name?" he replied.

"Hi. I'm Liz," I said as I took a seat and shook his outstretched hand.

"Hi. I'm Erik from the Netherlands. You've got to get some food, Liz. This place has the best food. But be careful not to pack on the pounds!" he continued as he spoke what I was already thinking.

I got up from my chair, waved at a few people staring at me from the other side of the table, and went inside the house to get dinner. The facility, in addition to its world-class clinicians, was known for its food and service, and they did not disappoint. Linens, china, silver, and crystal were everyday fodder here, and the meals were incredible. The first night I was there, I ate leg of lamb, couscous, roasted vegetables, crème brûlée, and sparkling water. After dinner, about twelve people stayed at the table to smoke and commune with each other. I was struck by how well they seemed to know each other and wondered how long they had been at the facility together.

Eventually, the group disbursed, and I headed back to my room. I felt oddly at home in my new locale, and I was excited at the prospect of actually getting better in body and spirit. I fell into bed, sunk into the luxurious sheets, hugged my pillow, said a prayer of thanks for finding this place, and had the best sleep I'd had in ages.

The weeks at the Malibu facility flew by. I met some cool people from all over the world, and the counselors and doctors were first-rate. Day by day, my mind cleared a little bit more, and the cobwebs disappeared somewhat from my brain. The dark thoughts and paranoia gradually lessened their grip on me, and I began to feel more hopeful about my future without being manic.

Chapter 79
More Bad News

When I arrived at the mansion, I had been told that I needed to go to the financial office and give them a credit card to cover what insurance didn't pay for my stay, which in the end was zero. I went to the office and handed my Platinum American Express card to the woman working there. She ran the card and let me know that it had been declined. Given that American Express doesn't have a spending limit and I had been told I was one of their top customers in the U.S., I was confused.

"Please try again," I urged.

She did, with the same results. I went to a house phone and called AmEx.

"Hello. My card has just been declined, and I don't know why," I said to the agent.

After we completed the usual security questions, most of which I answered incorrectly because they had been recently changed, the agent told me that he couldn't talk to me. He said that Joe had recently made himself administrator of my account and had taken me off. My AmEx had been deactivated and Joe had ordered new cards to be sent to him, not me.

"You have to be kidding me!" I said incredulously, with tears welling up in my eyes.

"I'm sorry, ma'am, but that is correct," he replied.

What ensued after that was practically a comedy as I fought with American Express for days to regain control of my account. What had happened became clear over time: while I was at UCLA, Joe had broken into the Airbnb where I was staying and stole my AmEx credentials, making himself the administrator of my account. Additionally, he had charged over $25,000 in bills to my account. American Express management initially said they were going to hold me responsible, but a year later, and with the help of an attorney, they correctly took off the charges.

Later, looking in detail at the charges he made on my account, it was clear what type of business Joe was really in: an escort service! All those people in his apartment on their computers were arranging for call girls to be driven to fancy hotels, with the transportation and hotel charges being billed to innumerable AmEx cardholders, including mine. Joe specialized in AmEx fraud. Fortunately, American Express did the right thing in my case, and I remain a fiercely loyal customer.

Chapter 80

Please, God, No

One day, toward the end of my stay in the Malibu mansion, I began to get ready for breakfast as usual. I showered, got dressed, and then decided to go to the bathroom before heading to the main house. When I stood up from the toilet, I felt lightheaded and a bit dizzy. As I turned around to flush the toilet, I gasped at the sight of a large amount of dark blood in the toilet bowl. This had come on without warning, and it was a total shock. Being a former doctor, I knew it couldn't be a good thing, but in my fragile condition, I knew I did not have the bandwidth to deal with it at that time. I quickly flushed the toilet, along with any worry about what I had just seen.

As part of the healing journey, this facility encourages visits from one's family. Given that my family was at a great distance, I was pleasantly surprised when my mother said she would come and visit me during my last week and join me in family counseling. The day before she was scheduled to arrive, I received a phone call from her letting me know she had just fallen and broken her hip and wouldn't be able to come for a visit.

Because of her condition, I elected to return immediately to Seattle upon discharge and provide support to my mother. It was also time for me to reconsider my plan to move to a warmer climate, as potential moves to Los Angeles and Las Vegas really hadn't panned out the way I had planned.

The day of discharge was bittersweet. I had become quite attached to the team of caregivers in this facility and had also made a few friends. With over twenty-five hours per week of intensive therapy, including EMDR and Reiki treatments, my time at the Malibu mansion had been the most prolonged and productive stint of my psychological life. I really didn't want to leave, but at a cost of $1,500 per day, I couldn't justify staying any longer.

My insurance denied payment for my stay in the Malibu mansion (after initially approving it while still in the hospital at UCLA) because I did not meet the criteria for drug or alcohol addiction, cut and dry. My illness, no matter how devastating, did not meet the criteria for benefits at this facility, so I paid for it myself. Fifty thousand dollars and thirty days later, I felt I really had received a significant benefit from the stay, but didn't want to continue to pay for treatment there.

The facility arranged for transportation back to LAX so I could fly home to Seattle. As I drove past all the familiar haunts in Malibu and Santa Monica, I didn't have the same fears and flashbacks this time. I was able to admire the incredible scenery without feeling so much shame, humiliation, and embarrassment. I promised myself that when

I returned to Los Angeles at some point in the future, I would do things differently, very differently. I vowed to return as a healthy, whole person, not the broken individual who had arrived previously.

My limo driver randomly shared with me that his fiancée had just been diagnosed with bipolar disorder, which I found to be a weird coincidence since I didn't mention my diagnosis to him. She was apparently where I recently was and was refusing to get help or acknowledge her situation. I felt sad for him, knowing what could lie ahead, and offered a few words of encouragement. The biggest message I gave to him was to not abandon her if he could avoid doing so. Bipolar disorder can be a very lonely experience, and the continued support of family and friends is essential to one's healing.

As the plane touched down in Seattle, I called my mom and said I would see her in a few hours. I arrived home, where I quickly took a shower and got ready to go see my mom at the hospital. I went to the bathroom before I left and had the same problem as I had in Malibu, only this time the blood was much worse. Given that I had a clearer head since the first time this happened, I realized that this could be a *real* problem. I assumed that, after all the stress I had been under, it was most likely an ulcer. But given how much blood I was potentially losing, I placed a call to my gastroenterologist's office.

I'm not sure if it is because I am a former physician and colleague, or if it were because I told them I had blood in the toilet, the office got me right in rather than the usual three-month wait. I headed to the same-day appointment with mild trepidation. Because it was a last-minute appointment, I was booked with a physician I had never seen before. He sat next to me and took a very detailed history. I'd had a colonoscopy with this group just eighteen months before this appointment and had been given a clean bill of health.

I knew a picture could be worth a million words, so I had taken a picture of the blood in the toilet to show the physician. As I pulled up the photo for him, I had a moment of complete lucidity and suddenly realized the medical gravity of what I was showing him. Suddenly, so much medical knowledge from the recesses of my mind started to come together, including my voracious appetite of late and unintentional weight loss.

The physician took the phone from my hands, enlarged the photo, and turned to address me directly. "Liz, you have colon cancer until proven otherwise."

"Colon cancer?" I asked incredulously. "But I had a clean bill of health from you guys less than two years ago!" I stated.

"Yes, I'm sorry. We must have missed the cancer during that colonoscopy. I'm going to admit you to the hospital tonight, and we will start our workup," Dr. Chow replied, looking very somber.

My mind raced with all the other diagnoses that could have been in play: ulcers, hemorrhoids, diverticulitis, diverticulosis, and so on. "Couldn't it be something else? Maybe it's gluten?" I begged.

"There's a ninety-nine percent chance this is cancer," he finished.

As I left the building to drive my car to the hospital, I reflected on how I had been told by Steve Jobs less than two years previously that I would get GI cancer, like him, if I didn't slow down and change my life. Even today, I cannot explain it.

Chapter 81

Life Goes On

It turned out that my diagnosis was indeed colon cancer. I was hospitalized and had surgery, followed by a brutal regimen of chemotherapy during COVID, which made it extra special. It became clear in 20/20 hindsight that my weight loss was a result of cancer and being in a hyper-metabolic state. I am now, and still, five years later, cancer-free.

After surgery and chemotherapy, I elected to stay in Washington and attend to my primary businesses there while launching my new ideas from Seattle. I decided to forego any more consultants for my new business and work directly with John from Houston. We continue to work with each other despite my more modest goals for my new company. John remains an important ally for me in business.

I heard from Jerry a few years after we first met. He had finally been able to get a phone and contact me. He decided, after many years of living on the streets of Malibu, to move to Park City. He was working at a ski resort and trying to put his life back together at age fifty-five.

He had reestablished contact with his children and was hoping to upgrade his bike for a car again one day soon. He was bunking with a new girlfriend in Utah, very happy to have a proper roof over his head.

I kept in touch with Scott over the past few years. He told me he decided to divorce Deborah after learning she was running an OnlyFans page using her naked son as a prop in her videos. He continues to work in Las Vegas real estate and is seeking full custody of his child. I sincerely hope he finds the woman he deserves.

I was eventually able to connect with David through Facebook. He called me on Messenger from a friend's phone and apologized profusely for getting my car impounded on the infamous cigarette run from Trump Tower. I apologized for his incarceration from the cigarette run. He indicated he had moved from the Las Vegas streets to the beaches of Los Angeles to be closer to the ocean and a few other homeless friends. Since our meeting at Trump Tower Las Vegas, he had been incarcerated numerous times, yet still refused any housing or help from anyone. He indicated he believes the world is soon coming to an end, and he would like to stay on the streets with "his" people in the meantime as he awaits the cataclysm.

I had lunch with Carl in Seattle a couple of years after standing him up after my debacle in Santa Barbara. He indicated he had no idea I was bipolar or manic when we had met and worked together over the past decade. He thought my hypercreativity and 'popcorn ideas' were par for the course in Hollywood. Likewise, he said it's common to be blown off in the entertainment industry, as I had done to him in Santa Barbara. When I shared with him that I am writing a book about my crazy time in California and Nevada, he asked for first right of refusal for the screenplay, and I look forward to our continued friendship and association.

Epilogue

One of the reasons I have written this book is to shed light on the insidious nature of bipolar disorder, which has a twenty-five percent incidence of death by suicide each year.

I functioned for decades with depression and mild mania, unaware I had a more ominous future ahead of me. I had taken my bursts of energy and lack of need for sleep in stride, never really thinking much about it. In fact, I believe my BPD helped propel me to success in my life, as needing little sleep was a very convenient thing during medical school and residency. It helped me build a career that was both rewarding and successful.

I have often described BPD as a life in a repeating cycle of ten parts of undetermined length. When you are normal, or hypomanic (the first eight parts), life is wonderful, and the opportunities are endless. People think you are charming and clever.

Then things start to go awry (the ninth part). Moods become darker, tempers become short, and the wheels start to come off in your life. You sever relationships, you overspend significantly, and you do stupid stuff (like dancing on a rooftop).

The tenth and final part in the cycle is when your world comes crashing down around you, and you are looking up to see bottom. During this time, many people lose their lives, get admitted to a psych ward, or end up in jail. Given that I had experienced two of those three things, I felt lucky that I hadn't lost my life, as I could have done so many times before.

As the BPD disease progresses, you may no longer have eight good parts in the cycle. Mania comes less frequently, and depression becomes a constant friend. Creativity, which is bountiful during hypomania and mania, all but disappears. What's left when mania leaves, if you're still alive, is usually quite troubling: debt, health problems, friendships and family in ruin, bank accounts emptied, and job losses.

As mania was leaving my body to be replaced by depression, it was always accompanied by shame, guilt, humiliation, and embarrassment. Oftentimes, helpful physicians will put the patient on antidepressants, which can exacerbate mania and BPD in the most awful way.

As you might imagine, I resisted the diagnosis of BPD before I finally came to accept it and admitted that the medication did make a difference. Bipolar disorder is often genetic (eighty percent), but no one in my family has this affliction. It is prevalent in women and men equally, and the average age of onset is twenty-one years old, with a peak from ages twenty to forty years old. But BPD is becoming more common in women aged fifty and above, as in my case.

BPD can be caused and brought on by trauma and traumatic events, and I certainly fit that category, beginning with the major head injury I sustained in the car accident at age seven. Stress, or a major life event that is stressful, can also bring on the disease. Prior to my diagnosis, I'd had stress in spades.

BPD is a trip, both factually and metaphorically. The overabundance of dopamine, the ingredient that causes mania, is the same substance released when consuming a drug such as cocaine. To be honest, the high from mania is like being on cocaine 24/7. But just as you can't survive on a steady diet of cocaine for a lifetime, so too can you not sustain the high from bipolar without suffering the consequences.

Dopamine in excess from BPD causes the same destruction to your body and psyche as drug addiction does and is just as lethal. And because the allure of the hypomania stage is so appealing, many bipolar patients do not stay on their medicine(s), relapsing just as a drug addict does. Truthfully, when it's your own body producing the high, it is hard to distance yourself from the source as you must do with cocaine or other drug addictions.

A major problem with the treatment of BPD is that many people do not want to take their medicine(s). Curbing one's dark side while simultaneously dampening creativity and energy is a hard pill to swallow, literally and figuratively. I resisted the diagnosis of mania for nearly two years with waxing and waning symptoms before I entered UCLA and finally accepted my situation.

To this day, years later and on medication, I feel dull and sharp as a spoon. But I willingly take my medication. I will not, and cannot, go back to the days of mania and depression. I think how I am on medication now is probably how most normal people are, in control of their emotions, behaviors, and thoughts. It is still a new world for me to feel 'normal.'

I do often reflect, however, on the fact that my disease, bipolar disorder, is identified by an overabundance of dopamine and as a mental illness. But Parkinson's disease, which is identified by a lack of dopamine in the brain, is considered a real medical problem in society and by the medical establishment. Why is that?

How did medicine as a profession delineate one disease as legitimate while the other is a mental deficiency wrought with prejudice, judgment, and discrimination? Do we blame the Parkinson's patient for their lack of dopamine? No! Then why do we treat *any* disease as a mental disorder? Mental illness *is* a medical illness! BPD is an organic disease of the brain, just like any other brain disease is. It is worthy of our serious attention and empathy. It is my mission to help change the perception of this complex disease, and it is time to do away with the term "mental illness."

Unmedicated BPD can destroy anything and everything in your life, and picking up the pieces can be *really* difficult. I have been incredibly fortunate to have the love and support of family and some friends throughout this ordeal. My oldest son and I have repaired our relationship to the point that I no longer get defensive when he asks me if I am taking my medication. I now see that he asks out of genuine concern for me. I know I am lucky to be alive, whether from cancer or

BPD, and I no longer take much of anything for granted in life. I know I am solely responsible for my mental health, and I gladly accept that challenge. A daily gratitude journal helps keep me grounded and focused on my present, not flights of future fantasy.

Healing from full-blown mania takes time, as the prolonged overdose of dopamine is toxic to the brain and body. It can sometimes take years, but it is possible. Medication, meditation, and therapy are all parts of living a life free from the ravages of BPD.

Today, safely almost five years away from my time spent at UCLA and the Malibu mansion, I remain stable, living and working a productive life without any of the ravages of BPD, albeit with a more realistic view of my life. I am still extremely goal-oriented, but I no longer have the accompanying angst and frenzy that can go with mania. With each passing day, I am stronger and more resilient, with optimism for my future. My family and I have thoroughly mended our fences, and we now enjoy a meaningful and mutually supportive relationship.

Am I glad for all I've been through? Yes, because it made me who I am today. If I hadn't lost my mind, I may not have ever found my soul.

Namaste.

About the Author

Liz Casper is a former medical doctor and first-time author. In her first work, she invites us into her world of unroofed thoughts and actions; subsequent diagnosis of bipolar disorder; and ultimate shattering of her world. Her story will leave you on the edge of your seat, yet hopeful. Through her brilliant storytelling, Casper brings awareness and compassion to a diagnosis that affects over 30 million people worldwide.

www.ingramcontent.com/pod-product-compliance
Lightning Source LLC
Chambersburg PA
CBHW051609120626
46551CB00014B/1730